SEIZING THE APPLE

Denise Lardner Carmody

SEIZING

THE APPLE

A Feminist Spirituality
of Personal Growth

Crossroad · New York

For Karla Kraft
A wise woman

1984
The Crossoad Publishing Company
370 Lexington Ave, New York, N.Y. 10017

Library of Congress Cataloging in Publication Data
Carmody, Denise Lardner, 1935–
Seizing the apple.
    1. Spirituality.   2. Feminism—Religious aspects—
Christianity.   I. Title.
BV4501.2.C316   1984   248.8'43   84-23693
ISBN 0-8245-0652-9

CONTENTS

PREFACE

I n recent years I have had quite a bit to do with women and men interested in spirituality—more precisely, interested in religious traditions as resources for a feminist lifeway that would have resonance and heart. These are the people I have had in mind while writing this book: students in courses such as "Women and Religion," people gathered by local chapters of the National Organization of Women (NOW), people I've met on the lecture circuit. I have pitched the book a little above what I would offer in such situations, so as to elicit reflections that might supply for a teacher's physical presence, but it is the same blend of theory and exemplification, mental forays and returns to earth, that I attempt in class situations. It is not, therefore, a book of pure research. It is a teacher's book, shaped by concrete experiences in several kinds of classrooms.

The book is shaped, as well, by my Christian faith. It tries, as did my book *Feminism and Christianity: A Two-Way Reflection* (Nashville: Abingdon, 1982), to maintain a twofold allegiance. I firmly believe that feminism, the commitment to women's full equalization with men, is a moral imperative, one of the most pressing of our time. I also firmly believe that, despite its patriarchal detritus, Christianity is a treasure-house of spiritual resources, a path that can lead straight to the loving God. Because I think that Christian faith is the heart of Jesus' matter, I feel free to make it the marrow of my spirituality. Because I see women's contributions as the next great evolutionary phase, I feel bound to join Christian faith to women's liberation. The result, I hope, is a centrism with something to say to at least 85 percent of both the Christian and feminist assemblies.

Last, a word about the title. I am not trying to encourage a prideful revolt against God. Insofar as the apple might stand for the divine will, I would want all children of Eve to seize it only as God directs. But I strongly believe that the apple of God's eye is the human being fully alive, stretching joyously toward his or her richest fruition. Thus I am trying to encourage all of Eve's children, but especially her daughters, to assert rigorously their talents for understanding and love. That, I believe, would greatly help us overcome the fall into impotence and triviality that so blights our current culture.

My thanks to Walter and Joann Wolski Conn for encouragement; to my husband John for editing and stronger turns of phrase; and to Karla Kraft, for more excellent typing.

1   *INTRODUCTION*

Twenty-five people—mainly youngsters about twenty, a few people over forty-five—hunch over their exams. We are half-way through RL 333: Women and Religion, and this makes me reflective. The course is going well. We are reaching the point where the students know one another well enough to speak up unselfconsciously and know me well enough to question and joke. The exam deals with materials from the world religions. By now the students know that no world religious tradition has much to brag about when it comes to how it has treated its women. Viewed by the anachronistic but none the less pressing standards of today's egalitarian instincts, Hinduism, Buddhism, Chinese religions, Japanese religions, Judaism, Christianity, and Islam have all sinned and fallen short of the glorious justice their best instincts dictate.

The second half of the course will deal with Christianity in more detail. Most of the students are Christian, so the second half of the course will bring more personal convictions and traumata into play. If the readings, lectures, discussions, and exams are not to produce a wholly negative impression, one mired in the churches' pervasive sexism, I will have to spotlight some hopeful, visionary aspects. What are these to be? How ought RL 333 to bring forth convictions that will lead to useful actions?

I've lived through this scenario four or five times since I arrived at Wichita State University to teach religion. Each time I offer Women and Religion some variant of the scenario unfolds as surely as the winter flu. At one time the study of women's experiences

1

with world religion might have been a curio, a sibling of the Ancient Artifacts course offered by anthropology, or the Coins and Treaties course offered by the history department. Today Women and Religion bristles with implications. The students—mainly women, but perhaps 10 percent men—inevitably have personal stories to narrate, some of them "heavy baggage." A dispassionate observer can see them connecting Gargi, the woman who confronts the Upanishadic seer Yajnavalkya, to their older sister (or mother or self) who confronted the local pastor. The Muslim views of paradise, with their flowing streams and buxom *hur*, bring half-amused, half-angry reactions: This is a post-*Playboy* generation, a group quite sophisticated about the manipulation of women as sex-objects. By the time we get to a fuller examination of Christian sexism and feminism, the pot is bubbling fiercely.

This pleases me, of course, for the beginning of any significant education is wonder, passion, personal involvement. If my students are to emerge with new treasures, insights that can justify the catalogue's hyperbole about "liberal" (freeing) education, they will have to get involved. On the other hand, the emotional intensity strains the scholarly part of me, which wants to be sure that complex realities get their due. It is somewhat fair to judge the past by what it has begotten in the present, but not wholly so. It is easy to underscore the gross disparagements of women that play through the writings of the Christian Fathers, but perhaps it is more important to estimate the liberations that embracing the Christian good news has made possible. So at this hinge-point of RL 333 I usually come down with a bout of reflection. How can I do justice to the scholarly demands of the materials, the detachment that higher education lauds, without doing injustice to the appetites I have aroused? What wisdom can I tease from the traditions that will redeem the heroic labors of their saints?

The resolution I have fashioned circles around "spirituality." The traditions that we study have been many things—cultural histories, philosophical systems, fascinating complexes of rituals, sociological laboratories—but at their core, in my view, they have been "ways to the center,"[1] living pursuits of saving wisdom. The passions of my students also are many things—childhood memories, economic grievances, bruises from bad marriages, worries about childrearing—but they too circle around a hunger to see and feel things in the round, holistically, in ways that would heal and elevate. In my lexicon "spirituality" is precisely this pursuit of saving wisdom, this hunger for healing and elevation. If people are not diminished to the status of computer cards, but are allowed to have three or more dimensions and think and feel, they show themselves to be spiritual: they are hungry to make sense of their experiences, and almost painfully eager to grow beyond their present impasses, to become strong and good.

Courses in the humanities that bypass spirituality as though it were improper for higher education condemn themselves to being merely academic. If teachers really want to educate, they must find a way—however disciplined, scholarly, or seemingly detached —to deal with what is real and pressing, both in the objective order that history and metaphysics reveal and in the anguish of the best students. My way has come to be trying to get students to see the religions as repositories of the human struggle for wholeness, centeredness, wisdom. In the second half of RL 333, this has come to mean testing the Christian propositions about *gratia sanans et elevans*: examining whether the love-life of the Christian God ("grace") can heal the slashes today's women suffer, can raise feminists (both female and male) to a dazzling vision of what ought to be, what they would sell all they own to have happen.

AN EXECUTIVE LUNCH

The students finish their exams, hand them over with sour or sweet faces that are fair predictors of their grades, and head off for their midterm break. I stuff their work into my pouch, gather up the day's mail, and head off for a luncheon meeting of the executive board of the women's studies program. The board meets twice a month to deal with long-range planning and put out brushfires. It brings together some of the liveliest women on campus, so I usually enjoy our gatherings. Today the topic is retrenchment contingencies —the plans the administration has for making cuts, should the state legislature announce a fiscal Armageddon is nigh. This is not the sort of topic that piques my appetite, but several of the board members are fine gallows-humorists, so I expect a few nicely barbed lines.

In the event itself, it turns out that I have underestimated the gloom of my fellow campesinas. I know that they think of themselves as existing only on sufferance, without any genuine support from the men who call the shots, but I have not realized the depth to which this feeling has eroded their confidence. As we break out our sandwiches, carrot sticks, yogurt, and the like, I hear tale after tale of foreboding. The program has a core faculty (small) who concentrate on women's studies courses in a strict sense, and a larger fantail of faculty like me who regularly focus on women's issues from other disciplinary standpoints. The core group, understandably, is the most depressed by the program's inability to progress toward gaining support in the upper echelons. Their heads are sore from banging against stone walls; they feel they are marching like Sisyphus. I listen for twenty minutes or so and then find myself daydreaming an arch little lecture.

"Sisters," I say, "I'm amused to have to tell you that your troubles are compounded by your lack of religious or, more precisely, theological sophistication. No, don't start to jeer and make those faces. I've been easy on you all this semester: This is my first lecture in six months. Today, however, the Holy Spirit and I have decided that your pagan souls cry out for a lecture on sin. So compose yourselves, sit tight, and pray that the Spirit gives me the charism of brevity.

"Sin: moral evil, culpable wrong-doing. The most salient characteristic of sin, from the viewpoint of those who believe in a good God and a good creation, is its irrationality. There is nothing to understand in sin. One gropes for the inverse insight that sin is a surd: a lack of proper reasonableness, a privation of the good will and love that ought to obtain. Sin is a closure against the light for which the human mind is made, a slamming of the door against the love that would make the householders whole. It is difficult to overestimate the pervasiveness of this surdity, and so it makes sense to speak of it as 'original,' something that has tilted the human game from the beginning. Where there should have been exchange, compassion, and collaboration, there has been aversion, silence, hardness, refusal to help. The parents have eaten sour grapes so, generation after generation, the children's teeth are set on edge.

"If you were less well read in *The New Yorker* and better read in the Bible, you would see your dilemma more accurately. *The New Yorker* says nothing about sin (except indirectly, through its opulent ads and its silence about grace and redemption). The Bible would teach you that stonewalling and rejection such as what you are running into is inevitable when people no longer wonder, watch, and pray. Your problem is those men's irreligion, their basic stuntedness. As well, the Bible would teach you that grace abounds over sin: the Mystery of life (God) is stronger than our closure, more loving than our pusillanimity. I know you don't cotton much to biblical language. If I only heard biblical language from the mouth of Jerry Falwell or Phyllis Schlafly, I wouldn't cotton to it either. But forget the well-worn phrases. Consider the realities. Until you name the enmity you are suffering, the aversion from Light and Love, you will not see it straight. Moreover, you will blame yourselves unfairly, and you will fail to see the campaign you should be mounting (naming the enemy accurately; showing with chapter and verse how your way is nobler, truer, more beautiful, more educational). That's my piece. Now I shall cease and desist. Be generous as the collection plate passes."

In my daydream, the sisters hiss and boo, but rather appreciatively. I know that many of them have been ill-treated by their churches, and they know that I am no defender of the irreligion that goes on locally most Sundays. But this is the first time I have imagined speaking to them in theological terms, or suggesting the view of human nature and grounds for hope that Christian faith holds out. This is the first time I have contemplated correlating feminist spirituality (which we have discussed in literary and political terms[2]) with Christian categories of faith. I'll have to consider whether acting on this daydream is prudent or foolhardy.

THE LONG SEARCH

It is Monday, the day that I teach 55 percent of my week's classes, so after a quick dinner I trudge out to my three-hour night class in comparative religion. To provide some oasis in what loomed as a desert of three hours of talk, I have scheduled films from a series entitled "The Long Search." It is a good series with an intelligent host, a competent board of scholarly advisors, and a fair treatment of the world's major religious traditions. Again and again, it shows the complexity in anything so mature as a "tradition" hundreds of years old. It also shows the centrality of spirituality. Tonight the film is on Islam, and once more I find my general estimates of the series verified.

The setting is Cairo, which is fortunate: I have been to Cairo and visited several of the sites the film shows. Not only can I nod sagely, I can also recall my own sense of grit and grandeur seeing gaunt men lost in prayer and pajama-clad kids risking their lives to hitch rides on the amazingly overcrowded buses. Cairo is something tactile for me—always a good thing for an interpreter of another culture or worldview. When the commentator enters the featured mosque, I can remember having my shoes wrapped in cloth coverings and feeling hands reach up to me for the expected alms. As we enter the darkened mosque and the light pours in through high, filigreed windows, I remember the startling effect of this juxtaposition of dankness and illumination. I used to think of a mosque as a place for bowing low and praying, a place of uncluttered space. Now I also think of it as a juxtaposition of light and dankness, of the need of human beings down low and the help of Allah breaking through up high near the ceiling.

My students include three young Malaysian girls who have come to Wichita (in one of the stranger dispensations of the gods of education) to study "secondary English," that is, how to teach English at the high-school level. They are devout Muslims, though they wear jeans rather than veils and giggle like any other freshmen. The class is fascinated at having in its midst people who actually follow what the people in the film believe, so they quickly start firing questions at the trio. The discussion finally comes round to the matter of the afterlife, and the most fluent of the trio gives the opinion that Muslims who sin will spend a considerable time in the Fire but then will be allowed entry to the Garden. "What about non-Muslims?" one of the more nervous Christians asks. "They will all go into the Fire, and for them there will be no escape."

This Christian only gets what he feared in his heart, so I don't feel too sorry for him. But I am astounded to hear this sophisticated young woman, who shows every sign of coping extraordinarily well in a foreign language and foreign culture ten thousand miles from home, come out with so stark and unnuanced a statement.

Later, she somewhat restores my faith in my ability to assess character, for after class I hear her asking the nervous Christian why he cares what another religion says will happen to him. But I find myself realizing again that spirituality needs years to oust dogmatism. Many of us are still clearing away simplisms, bogies, formulas learned by rote years ago.

The film saves Islam itself from simplism or rigorism, however, by portraying a remarkable couple, a chemistry professor and a physician, whose faith is a submission that mainly exalts the incomparable glories of God. The chemist is the man; for him the study of the Qur'an is so important that he has built his own mosque, where he presides twice a week at long study sessions with professional peers. The physician is the woman; she not only works in the government hospital but has been the moving spirit behind a private hospital that treats poor children afflicted with heart and pulmonary diseases. When this woman, who in the film looks to be about sixty, speaks of the imperatives in Islam to do good to one's neighbors, loving in all practical effectiveness such unfortunates as the indigent children her hospital treats, the Ayatollah Khomeini and his like who besmirch the Muslim image fade to insignificance. They will return, of course, when next the headlines speak of their having taken a thousand lives, but for the moment they are pygmies blocked out by a giant. The spirit of this woman, a believer and healer, is clothed with the sun. She is tough and she is gentle. Her face is lined with experience but her eyes are bright with wisdom. I would love to submit to the God who has fashioned so impressive a creature. Watching her go off on pilgrimage to Mecca, it is not at all hard to believe that there is no God but God.

I can't quite bring myself to speak with this diction to my students, but I do try to convey my respect. The advantage of The Long Search series is that it shows people of many faiths struggling admirably for wisdom and justice. Thus people of many faiths elicit my respect and, I hope, the respect of most of my students. Were the films to deal only with facts and figures, dates and doctrines, they probably would elicit markedly less respect. Since they deal with spirituality, faith forming concrete people, good and bad, they show the humanity of the world religions (allowing us to infer the inhumanity the traditions foster, when they cease to be spiritual). The search is long because it goes on all our lives, and because it has gone on since human beings first mourned their dead and worshiped what they found holy.

DEPTFORD AND WICHITA

Returned home from class, I pour a glass of port, put on some Vivaldi, and sink into my big chair. After a couple of minutes to let the whirl of images settle down, I pick up *World of Wonders*, the novel I have nearly finished. It has impressed me, so I find myself composing a tribute and appropriation: "Among the recent literary portrayals of the long search for wisdom throughout the life cycle, Robertson Davies' Deptford Trilogy[3] stands out for its depth and wholeness. Davies clearly has assimilated a lot of Jungian psychology, as well as literature and hagiography, which dispose him to think better of religion and the spiritual life than does the average contemporary novelist."

The main character in the trilogy, Dunstan Ramsay, is shaped decisively by his boyhood encounter with Mrs. Dempster, a strange sort of saint. Mrs. Dempster becomes bonded to Ramsay karmically when a snowball intended for him hits her in the head and causes her to give birth prematurely. This trauma somewhat unhinges her, bringing out a religiosity that scandalizes the little town of Deptford, Ontario, where they live. Two aspects of this religiosity snap me to attention. The first is Mrs. Dempster's lack of fear. Some part of her has such close contact with God that she refuses to kowtow to any lesser force. Thus when Dunstan visits her before going off to fight in World War I she gives him a remarkable parting gift: "When I had to leave she kissed me on both cheeks—a thing she had never done before—and said, 'There's just one thing to remember; whatever happens, it does no good to be afraid.'"[4]

The second aspect of Mrs. Dempster's religiosity that impresses me is her freedom, which is the other side of her lack of fear. She becomes ostracized by the townfolk of Dempster because of her behavior with a wretched tramp. As reported by Dunstan, who had joined the search party that formed when Mrs. Dempster was found missing:

"I made a sound—I am sure it was not a yell—that brought my father beside me in an instant. He shot the beam of his flashlight into the scrub, and in that bleak, flat light we saw a tramp and a woman in the act of copulation. The tramp rolled over and gaped at us in terror; the woman was Mrs. Dempster. It was Hainey who gave a shout and in no time all the men were with us, and Jim Warren was pointing at the tramp, ordering him to put his hands up. He repeated the words two or three times, and then Mrs. Dempster spoke. 'You'll have to speak very loudly to him, Mr. Warren,' she said, 'he's hard of hearing.' I don't think any of us knew where to look when she spoke, pulling her skirts down but remaining on the ground. It was at that moment that the Reverend Amasa Dempster joined us; I had not noticed him when the hunt began, though he must have been there. He behaved with great dignity, leaning forward to help his wife rise with the same sort of protective love I had seen in him the night Paul was born. But he was not able to keep back his question. 'Mary, what made you do it?' She looked him honestly in the face and gave the answer that became famous in Deptford: 'He was very civil, 'Masa. And he wanted it so badly.'"[5]

In retrospect, toward the end of his life, Dunstan Ramsay considers this the first of three miracles (the tramp became a great benefactor of the poor) that Mary Dempster wrought. As Ramsay is a hagiographer and so familiar with criteria for canonization, he counts her a saint. The other two miracles were her reviving his brother Willie from death and her appearing in a vision when Dunstan was lying wounded on a battlefield in France. Ever after the vision, Mary Dempster was a gentle pressure on Ramsay to keep the world alive with wonders, never to underestimate the holy and mythic forces that twine around what is most creative, vital, and human in us. The trilogy is a lush forest, with many paths besides the narrative about Mary Dempster, but she is one of its most striking beauties. So I sip my port and wonder about her spirituality, asking myself whether Deptford, or Wichita, could ever have appreciated her. Indeed, would saintliness be at home in any of our cities—in any place where self-serving mores or economic profits call the cultural tunes?

We have to transcend selfishness and narrowness if we are to unfold our wings and take flight. We have to die to convention, as much in ourselves as in our town, if we are to follow the Spirit of

Christian spirituality. These are familiar notions backed by verses one can quickly find in the New Testament, in John of the Cross, or other masterworks. Somehow, though, they take flesh and become more palatable, more possible, when one contemplates such an ordinary extraordinary person as Mary Dempster.

My husband's aunt, a nurse for forty-five years, lived in a tiny hospital apartment as happily as if she had been a queen in a castle. She complied with all her generation's outward forms, appeared quite conventional, yet now and then showed amazing streaks of freedom. For example, when she found that she had a serious stomach disorder, probably cancer, a voice inside kept her from going to the doctor. She had seen too many people wasted by chemotherapy to consider that an imperative or attractive option. So she made her peace with God, went about her business, and took to her bed only when the sickness finally overpowered her. She was not afraid of death, and she was almost angrily free of our contemporary compulsion to mechanize the last weeks of dying. Her time had come. It would do no good to delay it by gimmickry.

I keep returning in memory to the light this freedom sheds on the contentment and generosity of Aunt Catherine's prior years. At work, in family gatherings, among her friends, she was always quiet, agreeable, dependable, and utterly generous. At Mass each morning before the sun had cleared the horizon, she was always bowed low in prayer. A good spirituality would help us to live well by teaching us how to die well. A good spirituality would so bind us to God that we would stand free of the all-too-human conventions of a Deptford, a Wichita, an anywhere.

THIS BOOK

This book is, first, a work on spirituality. My hope is that it will depict the Christian tradition as a viable, attractive way to wisdom and wholeness today. My focus, therefore, is not doctrinal, historical, or ethical. Those aspects of the Christian faith may come into play, but they will be subordinate to a focus on bringing the tradition alive, making the Spirit of Christ imaginable. How original the work will turn out to be is not an important consideration. My experience has been that whenever something significant dawns, something true at any depth, it seems orginal.

I see myself, through days such as the one I sketched in the Introduction, as groping toward this sort of originality. In the classroom, with my colleagues, at my sources, I keep turning the materials, old and new, this way and that, searching for the angle that
would make them prismatic. For twenty-five years I have been a
teacher, a manipulator of prisms. One does not turn that off when
the typewriter starts to hum. One simply tries to lay out the columns of ideas, create the frictions and sparks through another
medium. Further, just as I try in the classroom to stand as a colleague of my students in a common search for the living wisdom of
the religious traditions, so I shall try here to constitute myself a
colleague or collaborator of the reader. We are in this long search
together; I am simply handing over ("traditioning") what I have
seen, thought, glimpsed, hoped—because a few other searchers
may find it useful.

Second, this book is a feminist work. By that I mean that it stands
in the widening stream of searches that feel the past neglect of
women's contributions to the canonical views of Christian wisdom
to be noxious and feel the present burgeoning of women's contributions to be God-given. When half of any population is neglected,
that population is bound to limp along. The Christian population
of women has been egregiously neglected in all matters of official
teaching and leadership. Thus, it is not surprising that the Christian population ("the church") as a whole has been limping more
and more painfully. Because we have been on the margins of official church culture, and often have been victims of a thoughtless
church brutality, women have amassed a store of spiritual resources whose time to shine may well have come. When so many
old verities have broken down, so many legalisms been shown
impotent, the subtler, more primordial paths that have preserved
women's sanity and been ways to survive stand forth as encouraging signs for hope. Were women to get a serious hearing in the
boardrooms of Washington, Detroit, on Madison Avenue and
other power spots, two-thirds of the spiritual deadliness hanging
over those power spots like a lethal mist could be blown away. I
look forward to trying to think out on paper, as I have been trying
to think out in the classroom, the forms this ecological restoration
could take. As well, I am eager to paint the positive alternatives to
pollution that feminist spiritual theologians are fashioning. It is
not doctrinaire loyalty that moves me to name this work "feminist,"

then, but a conviction that many of the grassroot communities presently richest in the inspiration of Christ's Spirit are covens where women's wisdoms speak freely.

Third, the operative figure in this work of feminist spirituality is "self-transcendence." This is a figure I borrow from Bernard Lonergan, on whom I wrote my doctoral dissertation in philosophy. The term in my imagination suggests a person pushing aside barriers, tollgates, and entering new realms. In this case, though, the new realms are hitherto unexplored and unutilized parts and capacities of the self. The self is not isolated or solipsistic, so the realms often are social—borders with other people and talents shared with fellow travelers. Equally, the self is not simply active. It does not develop, grow, and mature to the measure Christ has in mind by a straight linear progress. Often the transcendence that brings the richest growth in faith and spirituality is a form of suffering, of letting go, stumbling in darkness. So I do not see this work as another bit of cheery self-help, more pages on lengthening your arms to pat your back. Rather, I see it as an exploration of the ways feminist insight suggests we reconceive the image of self-transcendence through what Christian maturity means today.

In organizing my thoughts about a feminist sprituality centered by self-transcendence, I have decided to begin with speculative matters and then proceed to practical matters. Thus chapters two, three, and four will be efforts to recast and extend the ideas of other spiritual theologians I find helpful. After an Interlude to sum up where I think these efforts have brought us, I shall try in chapters five through eight to apply my viewpoint, the feminist self-transcendence I have worked out, to the main concerns of the women in my classes, their prayer, work, family life, and politics. Obviously, I can give none of these concerns a full and adequate treatment. But by the time we reach chapter nine, the summary and conclusion, I hope to have presented a comprehensive point of view. If I have succeeded, and the reader has come to share my outlook, further applications to economic policy, war-making, sexual morality, church ministry, and the like should be relatively easy.

2 _____ *A VISION*

T he book that has moved me most deeply since I've started consciously to grope after a feminist spirituality focused on self-transcendence is Rosemary Haughton's *The Passionate God*. Passage after passage cries out for grateful and seconding commentary, but let me begin with a reference to feminine wisdom. Haughton has been speaking of the newer, freer church that the breakup of pre–Vatican II culture is calling forth, and of the wider symbolisms that the eucharist and the Christian ministry are taking on:

> This shows the fluid quality of the signification that goes on, and people learn, without realizing they are learning, to live their being as body of Christ in their bodies, as bodies becoming spiritual, as spirit articulated in body. Wisdom is incarnate in this newly-born Church which knows itself, more clearly than it has ever done, as the Grail, the feminine physical vessel of vision, which is no merely passive container but the vital, particular human body which is full of Christ. This is where the beginning of the End has to be, as it was at the beginning of incarnation, and as it was at the beginning of creation itself, when Wisdom "covered the earth like a mist." From the feminine principle comes all life, but now the feminine is not goddess but both human and divine, the son from the mother and the mother in the son, clearly, consciously, particularly, men and women who are in their particularity the body of Christ. As she comes to consciousness and to clearer and clearer articulation, so he grows towards his full stature. As he reaches "from

glory to glory" becoming more and more clearly himself in his earthly body, so the passionate desire of the bride for her lover reaches out to his passion for her, and they will no longer be denied.[1]

First, the place where Christians, or all people for whom Christ is a valid symbol of human perfection, live is the body of Christ. As Saint Paul did, we must take seriously this "location" of our lives. In the body of Christ the signs we use to convey our deepest hopes and fears signify beyond what we may realize. So, for example, a mother comforting her child against the dark is embracing the child with the protection of God, with the last shelter all of us have against the darknesses of sin, death, meaninglessness, and hell. A friend sharing a meal with a friend is communicating in the posture of God, who diffuses being, grace, the love-life of heaven so constantly that we take it for granted. Mainly unawares, we grow familiar with the mysterious economy of grace into which our bodies insert us. The Spirit of the loving Mystery of God expresses itself in our bodies, making them more "spiritual": symbolic, transparent, conductive. The holistic wisdom of God that is the sense and direction of all vitality, all life in the spiritualized body, takes form in the collectivity of Christ's members, all those who even stumblingly follow him. So the church, the "gathering" (*ecclesia*) of the members, is the prime receptacle or Grail of the vision that sees God's presence here, now, not apart from the world but ingredient, incarnate in the world. The members, sung and unsung, official and marginal, are in their togetherness full of Christ—are the extension and ongoingness of the incarnation of the Logos.

Second, the body of Christ is where the end, the consummation, the fulfillment for which all creation groans begins. The body of Christ began the enfleshment of God's visionary speech. It was in God's mind in the beginning of creation, for all creation holds together in the Word that took flesh and lived among us. The Wisdom of God that played before him at the foundations of the world, that covered the earth like a mist when creation first took form, is the feminine principle of life, wholeness, of understanding too deep and full to be expressed in angular, sharp, dichotomizing, either-or modalities. The feminine principle of wholeness issues all life, which comes forth small and fragile but whole.

Since the historical Christ, however, the feminine principle is clearer than it was when goddesses and androgynes stood the prime symbolic duty. Christ as feminine wisdom incarnate is human as well as divine, the juncture of the two-way exchange between humanity and divinity. In the relations that flow between Christ the Son and Mary the Mother, Haughton sees an epitome of the exchange of love between God and the world that is the world's creation and salvation. The son takes his life from the mother, and the mother of this son who incarnates divine wisdom finds her full life in the whole body of the body she has brought forth.

Third, we today have the chance to know these things, be these things, deal in this economy, clearly, with awareness, in all our individuality and specificity. It is Martha and Mary, Rudy and Whitey, real and normal individuals who flesh forth the divine wisdom and articulate into the body of Christ. As the church, Christ's bride, becomes more aware of this identity, the Christ grows toward his full stature, that end point where God will be all in all. He passes from splendor to splendor not in some distant heavenly sphere but in the painful progressions of his earthen, lumpy, unsplendid body. And this process is the passion, the holy eros, of a bride for her lover. Indeed, for Haughton history is the passion, now admitted now repulsed, of the bride for her lover, the passion of the minds and hearts made for wisdom, for the Wise Word that would set them free, give them perfect increase. At the end, which has been in labor since the resurrection, there will be no more frustration and denial. At the end, Lady Wisdom will shine as though clothed with the sun, fulfilled in the consummation of the passion of Christ and his bride.

EXCHANGE

The flow of love, the passion, that gives history its axis came to Western consciousness in the breakthrough of romantic love in the South of France toward the eleventh century. This romantic tradition gave the West, and through the West the world, a vocabulary by which it might deal with the experiences that most directly crack open God's nature. Haughton's prime example of romantic love explored in depth is Dante's *Divine Comedy*. In the figure of Beatrice, Lady Wisdom leads the receptive poet to the heights of understanding how God is love. St. Francis of Assisi, a troubadour of God in the romantic tradition, has become perhaps the best loved of the saints because of his joyous, stripped, utter passion for his God and Savior. Even though the Dantes and Francises are bound to be rare, they have made an indelible mark on human awareness. In their aftermath it is hard to avoid the ecstatic experiences of romantic passion for God, the implications of romantic passion for the exegesis of God's ways with human beings. As peak, nonpareil venturings of the human spirit, the poems of Dante and the songs of Francis give nearly incomparable meaning to the traditional notion that human beings are images of God. If we can love as these romantic heroes have, it is less incredible that God so loved the world he gave his only begotten son for the world's salvation.

Haughton's guide through the thickets of romantic love is the British writer Charles Williams.[2] A key concept in Williams' application of romantic love to Christian salvation-history is "exchange." Haughton uses this concept to describe both the triumphs of grace and the triumphs of sin. When grace, God's love and personal life, finds openings in human personalities or situations, it establishes an exchange, a flow, a commerce that proceeds heart to heart. People are brought to see the world as it really is, through the eyes of the Lover who made it. A certain connaturality, the scholastics would have called it, comes about, so that recipients of God's grace take on features and qualities of the divine nature. This accords with the rather cryptic lines in 1 Peter 2:3–4: "His divine power has granted to us all things that pertain to life and godliness, through the knowledge of him who called us to his own glory and excellence, by which he has granted to us his precious and very great promises, that through these you may escape from the corruption that is in the world because of passion, and become partakers of the divine nature."

In this quotation "passion" means untoward desires, not the romantic longing for a pure, ecstatic union with the beloved, human or divine. The punch line, however, is the last phrase, "become partakers of the divine nature." Were Paul to have written the passage, he probably would have referred to the body of Christ, but the meaning would have been the same. By God's grace, God's incalculable power, any who open their souls to noble love become joined to God, at one with God, assimilated to what God is.

Conversely, any who close themselves to noble love block the exchange that is at the heart of salvation, the center of God's design to secure human beings their fulfillment. This closure or blockage, this refusal to exchange, is what we mean by sin. As noted in the first chapter, it is utterly, essentially irrational. Yet it is as pervasive and destructive as all the places in past human history, all the zones of present human social existence, where irrationality and lovelessness preside: the wars and arms race, the unjust economic structures, the unnecessary suffering (starvation, illiteracy, drug abuse), the oppression of peoples of color and women, and so on and on. These are all places where exchange is refused. In each and every one of them people disobey the command we both know intuitively and find to be the epitome of Jesus' message. People are not willing to love the Lord, their God, with whole mind, heart, soul, and strength. They are not willing to love their neighbors as themselves. Therefore they ligate the tubes, the conduits, that would bring them the divine love. Therefore they reject the one power that can create life and repair it.

Haughton does not speak in the Teutonic tones of Karl Rahner, another of my beloved tutors, but she expresses in poetic and feminist language the radical cut Rahner has made to the heart of Christian and human matters.[3] For Rahner, a fundamental option lies before all human beings, a basic confrontation that calls them to say yes or no to the Mystery as which God comes. If they say yes (and they may do this largely unawares, in the wellsprings of the heart that speech may interpret badly), they open themselves to the love that moves both them and the stars, making possible Williams' and Haughton's "exchange." If they say no (and we hope that few say a radical no), they break off the exchange and wander bereft of their lifeline. The many evidences of refusal, naysaying, broken connection, and wandering say that sin is nothing trivial. It may be incomprehensible, on the level of rational analysis, but it is a powerful player in almost all our human situations. Still the cunning of God's love keeps trying to find weak points, chinks in the walls of refusal, through which it may enter. Crises in personal life or the death throes of historical periods offer times when even the stubbornest human beings may lessen their opposition to opening, and entertain the possibility that there is a God eager to help and able to save.

SIN

I have been saying that Lady Wisdom, the feminine sense of the whole of God's love and realism, spotlights the paramount value of exchange. It is by sharing with God and one another that we allow the divine passion for our well-being to work. As the rules of this exchange are not so rigid or derivative as the codes of a canon or penal law, so the sanctions for refusing this exchange are not so superficial. Sin warps the sinner, injures the refuser, taking the bloom from her life. This does not deny the social outreach of sin, the sinner's responsibility for the suffering others undergo because of her refusal. It simply begins at the beginning, which is her mysterious, impenetrable refusal to go where reason dictates, follow the best instincts of her heart. Thus the sinner ought to be for us a figure summoning compassion. When we can get beyond our anger at the wreckage the sinner causes, we can glimpse how Jesus could beg the Father to forgive his persecutors, because they did not know what they were doing.

A second reason for dealing with sinners compassionately is the large quantity of sin that now is impersonal, structural, a wicked legacy from past history. We all now live, move, and have our being in societies that have been warped and thrown out of joint by generations of closure. In every town on the face of the earth exchange is less than it should be, closure more than it need be. So a daughter in her mid-thirties engaging her seventy-year-old mother for the first time over the trials and tribulations of the mother's long life finds it hard to cast many stones. The sufferings of the daughter's childhood remain, as scars somewhat traceable to the mother's responsibility. But the daughter now sees the tangledness of that responsibility, the many lets and hindrances to the mother's freedom when the mother was the daughter's present age, and for the first time she moves to embrace her mother in compassion. Behind this mother is a grandmother equally scarred, equally a transmitter of disorder, confusion, a sense of worthlessness, and the like. To the side are an alcoholic father, a passive grandfather, and kids (the daughter herself, a brother) who have been less than perfect lovers. All of these have not done many goods they should have done, have done many evils they should not have done. All of us are sinners, by context and personal choice alike. Thus all of us draw from God, who knows our tangled skeins to their least knots and bulges, a heartfelt, motherly compassion. God is eager to forgive us our trespasses, hungry to wash away our transgressions in a wave of compassion, for God knows our ignorance of what we do.

The body of Christ has been most beautiful when it has shown such compassion to its suffering sinners. It has been most ugly when it has subordinated such compassion to rules, laws, or power plays. The Lady Wisdom, Sophia, who would move the church by the Spirit, would always have the body love the spirit more than the letter. The Lady Wisdom constantly would remind the body that God's love stands by, eager to heal, make new beginnings, and save. The best moments in pastoral theology occur when theologians turn this base line of Christian faith to practical account.

For example, the German theologian Walter Kasper, writing about the pastoral problems of contemporary Christian marriage, has recently said:

> Jesus proclaimed the God of human beings; his proclamation of the indissolubility of marriage was not a killing law but a word of life and salvation. His message is therefore an obligation to the Church to care for existing marriages, both those that are safe and those that are threatened. This also includes legal protection. If the Church's law in the Spirit of Christ is a law of mercy, then it is also essential for the Church to question itself again and again to make sure if it is doing justice to people in all the difficult and complex situations in which they find themselves in the modern world or whether it is not helping them in those situations. It may, for example, be an obstacle to their conversion and reconciliation, rejecting them hurtfully instead of giving them human and Christian support. A revision of canon law might well help, for instance, in the many cases in which there was, according to contemporary psychological insights, no full act of personal consent to the marital contract because the partners were lacking in maturity, to open the way to an annulment of such marriages.[4]

In the tangles of a broken marriage, both structural sin and personal sin mount a case for compassion. People have seen less clearly, been more self-serving, than what was necessary for a full, healthy, flourishing Christian marriage. Their surrounding society has led them, like wolves herding sheep, into false temples of money, pleasure, and status. The church has stood aloof from where they have lived their real spiritual lives, from what has been molding their innermost hearts. But the Spirit has not been aloof, for the Spirit is the love poured forth by the God who has not left himself without witness anywhere. So the Spirit has been making a prayer, with sighs too deep for words, in the hearts of all who have felt afflicted by sin, confused and contorted. The wise word that Lady Wisdom inspires, to keep some clarity despite sin, insists on objective things like the ideal of an indissoluble marriage. But the passionate, romantic love of God is more interested in exchange than ideals, so, with the Lady's blessing, under the Lady's urging, the love of God seeks ways to break through the most sinful of marital or other situations and reestablish communion.

GRACE

The grace of God that exchange allows to work often shows itself the most powerful, holistic, and maturing force around by its ability to marry objective ideals to existential compassion. It is not at all simplistic, but as subtle and demanding as what wisdom finds each situation to need. Thus, to follow up on Kasper's example of annulment, I recall a couple who were married close to ten years and then, at the man's instigation, separated and divorced. Five years later the woman received a visit from a priest who was investigating the possibility that the couple qualified for an annulment. The priest was on his mission at the urging of the former husband, who wanted to marry again. This was the first the woman had heard of any annulment. In the woman's eyes, the couple had been well aware of what they were doing when they married at age twenty-two, and their two good-sized children were ample evidence that the marriage had been consummated. Her judgment was that the marriage had simply broken down. There had been a marriage (for seven or eight years they had been quite happy), but gradually, for complex reasons, it had frayed and then completely come apart. To say that there never had been a marriage, as the priest was trying to say, offended the woman deeply. It mocked the children in her house and tainted the good years she was trying to retain in her memory as the basis for continuing to believe in the fidelities of marriage and faith. But the woman's testimony had no effect on the investigatory process. Some months later she received in the mail notice that her marriage had been annulled and that she and her former husband were free to marry.

So, despite the advances in Kasper's proposals over the previously rigid views of marital indissolubility, the recent broadening of the grounds for annulment to include psychological immaturity has its own problems and pitfalls. Insofar as it still proceeds casuistically, whittling finer and finer distinctions, the new reform misses the point, just as did the old inflexibility. The point is an honest, straightforward dealing with bare realities so that they may be moved toward healing by God's love. To me, who knew the couple quite well, the priest's work was a rather shabby game-playing. It was not my part to inquire whether the former husband petitioning for the annulment had told the priest of his several adulteries and affairs. It was not my desire to obstruct either partner's chances for future happiness. It was my feminine instinct, however, that, as so often happens with canon law, sterotypically male rigidities were twisting a complex reality out of shape. Surely good will and imagination could have found a way to honor both the reality of the old marriage and the equal reality of its breakdown. Surely the Spirit who interprets things such as Jesus' reported sayings about marriage could have correlated these with Jesus' other reported sayings about freedom and come up with a fairer, more loving resolution. To my instinct, the problem was that the Spirit was never consulted.

An important part of Rosemary Haughton's credibility is her constant inclination to the both-and, her regular ability to join justice and compassion. In her case good will and an exceptional imagination fashion creative solution after creative solution. So, for example, after discussing the bodily symbolisms of the hand and the generative organs, and frankly acknowledging that sexuality can refuse exchange as well as mediate it, Haughton speaks of relating precise moral judgments to God's ability to break into even sinful situations:

What I want to outline here, for others to fill in, is simply the way in which an understanding of body symbolism as discovered in the way of exchange shows us simultaneously the possibility of true and precise moral judgment and decision and also (at the same time and by the same criteria) the glorious ruthlessness of divine love in finding a way to give itself in a bodily situation distorted by sin. Truthfulness and compassion, clarity of judgment and tenderness of action, are not opposites but two results of the same vision. This was how Jesus saw things. His demands were as absolute as heaven and hell, but that very fact made him furiously tender to the damaged and the weak and the muddleheaded. It is only by striving in all humanity to see things as he did that his Church can be faithful to the stringency of his demands and the delicate sensitivity of his discernment of love's way in a sinful situation.[5]

And just what is love's way in a sinful situation? I think it boils down to proclaiming and acting upon the abounding of grace over sin. This is at the center of Paul's proclamation, as he compares Adam and Christ:

If, because of one man's trespass, death reigned through that one man, much more will those who receive the abundance of grace and the free gift of righteousness reign in life through the one man Jesus Christ. Then as one man's trespass led to condemnation for all men, so one man's act of righteousness leads to acquittal and life for all men. For as by one man's disobedience many were made sinners, so by one man's obedience many will be made righteous. Law came in, to increase the trespass; but where sin increased, grace abounded all the more, so that, as sin reigned in death, grace also might reign through righteousness to eternal life through Jesus Christ our Lord. (Romans 5:17–21)

I do not doubt that fancy footed exegetes can read this passage in ways that would prevent our speaking of grace's abounding over sin at the foundations of every situation we encounter. I also do not doubt that Lady Wisdom rejects such readings, plumping for the application in all situations of the core ratio at the center of the message of Paul and all the evangelists: the ratio of resurrection to death. If Jesus was raised, grace abounds over sin. If Jesus was raised, every situation has present the resources of a God whose will to save is the strongest force, the most wily creativity, there ever has been.

CHURCH

The Body of Christ, Paul's church, is inconceivable apart from the resurrection. Physically, it is the resurrection that frees Jesus from the bonds of a limited corpus and makes him the Christ, the Messiah who can be the head of an extended body, a corps of lovers who stand together in sight of the End. Spiritually, it is the resurrection that gives the many fragile branches the major symbol that lets them believe they are inseparably joined to the vine. If Christ is not risen, Pauline faith is in vain. If Jesus is not deathless, the Johannine branches have nothing sure in which they can abide. The church is gathered by the Spirit of Jesus' resurrection. It goes forth on mission to all nations because it has good news no eye has previously seen, no ear has previously heard, the human heart has not previously conceived: God's having reached into time and drawn a fully human brother of ours up into the eternal life of the divine community of love.

"Fine, another sweet little purple patch," the more pragmatic among you may be saying. Readers of Rosemary Haughton, however, quickly find themselves won over to the necessity and pragmatism of poetry, patches purple with the wine of Christ's victory. For it is only poetically that we can even stutter about the mystery of God, the vision of Lady Wisdom. The language of the Spirit is evocative, sacramental. One cannot even hear this language without a touch of poetic inspiration.

Another poetic way of describing the church, Christ's Body, would be: people so seized by the Spirit of love that they regularly live in the whole, at the foundations. These people would cut across the lines we presently draw among Protestants, Catholics, and Orthodox. They would not be limited to explicit Christians, and they would turn out to be a strange collection of bedfellows. For the truth, in Lady Wisdom's perspective, seems to be that all peacemakers are children of God, all who are moved by the Spirit and cry, "Abba." If Elie Wiesel is not a member of God's church, then I don't know where to locate God's church. True enough, Wiesel is so resolutely a Jew that he might reject membership in any "church," and distinctions among Christians and Jews, Hindus and atheists, continue to have some utility. This utility lessens, however, in the measure that we approach the End, point Omega. The approach by way of nuclear devastation is a hellish road, but if that is where we find ourselves, let it be nuclear perils that reveal the at best penultimate, in fact the rather trivial character of our distinctions. The approach by way of new social organizations, groups that give some sign of building into what Teilhard de Chardin called the "hyperpersonal," is more joyous and fitting, and it too soon breaks down the walls between Jews and Gentiles, those who confess God with their tongues and those who only confess God with their good deeds (the "good atheists").

But just where might such new social organizations be? They might dot the landscape of many lands, already be set in place and reticulating toward one another, if we put a new lens in our glass. Consider the 100,000 *comunidades de base* already humming in Brazil.[6] Consider the grassroots communities that already meet, quietly but to the sustenance of millions, in North America and Europe. Look to the political cells that are joining people against nuclear weapons, racial discrimination, sexual oppression, economic injustices, and the like. Are all these groups not cells of the Body of the Word of the God who wants human beings to survive, come together, love one another? Is it realistic to separate their evolutionary significance from the cosmic Christ that Paul and John glimpsed at the start of the Christian gospel? I think it cannot be realistic to make such a separation. I think Christ must be growing wherever people are resurrecting hope from despair.

HOLISM

"We distinguish in order to unite," was the venerable dictum of *philosophia perennis*. Through the ages, lovers of wisdom have known that the most careful analyses must remain in the service of synthesis if learning is not to move people away from the understanding that gives life. Because our time is sated with analysis, I stress synthesis. Because the masculine intelligence that prevails today is obsessed with distinguishing, I stress unifying. And how does one unify? By having a holistic sense of the foundation, the lever, the apple of God's eye.

I have been suggesting that the foundation is the Resurrection, but I could as well have suggested grace, love, the Spirit, or the sacramental Christ. Each of these major Christian symbols, if deeply plumbed, leads into the Mystery that integrates the whole. This is the Mystery that hushes the mind, solicits the heart, makes contact at what the mystics call "the fine point of the soul" (*scintilla animae*). It is the God who comes in a cloud of unknowing to teach us that in the order of grace love precedes knowledge. In other orders love follows upon knowledge, but when we come to grace, the order that we enter by conversion to God's standards, knowledge follows upon love. The love of wisdom that genuine philosophy attains is a sense of the whole, the ecological and organic entity that the unknowings of the cloud bring into clearer relief.

Maria Theotoky, one of the best named symbols of Lady Wisdom to enter upon the literary scene in many years, puts this feminine orientation toward holistic understanding in the following terms: "It is not that I wanted to know a great deal, in order to acquire what is now called expertise, and which enables one to become an expert-tease to people who don't know as much as you do about the tiny corner you have made your own. I hoped for a bigger fish; I wanted nothing less than Wisdom. In a modern university if you ask for knowledge they will provide it in almost any form—though if you ask for out-of-fashion things they may say, like the people in shops, 'Sorry, there's no call for it.' But if you ask for Wisdom—God save us all! What a show of modesty, what disclaimers from the men and women from whose eyes intelligence shines forth like a lighthouse. Intelligence, yes, but of Wisdom not so much as the gleam of a single candle."[7]

Intelligence only becomes wise when it is willing to venture broadly and deeply. Wisdom is not content to master only a tiny corner. She must parade through the entire marketplace, shouting the preeminence of her wares. Not for her the straitjackets of disciplinary expertise. These would be fine were they to do their work and then place themselves in the service of a bigger picture, a view "under the aspect of eternity." But their tendency is to be far more prideful. Not only will the disciplines not play a subordinate role, they usually deny that there is any such thing as a bigger picture, an aspect of eternity. So narrowness becomes a lapel button of pride. Disciplinary arcaneness becomes a badge of honor, something inaccessible to the vulgar hordes. And then the more egregious of the overly specialized universities prate about things like "quality of mind," when they want to exclude from their inner sanctums (tenure) those of feminine bent who insist that life only flourishes in the whole, that a university ought to be, as its name suggests, a place where knowledge is under constant pressure to come together and point toward a unity.

Holism, of course, pertains to much more than the university and the life of the mind. It pertains even more primordially to the unity of mind and body, which is the privileged focus in any medicine, education, or religious devotion that knows its business. In sociological terms, holism is the force that keeps the many disparate groups and subgroups from forgetting the prior unity of the whole *res publica*. True enough, it is good for a country not to melt down its ethnics, important for each native group to keep a sense of itself. But when such a sense militates against the common good of the whole (especially the common good of the whole citizenry of the one planet), it becomes vicious. Erik Erikson has called such a vicious ethnocentrism or nationalism a "pseudospeciation," suggesting that it somewhat deliberately tries to blink the stark biological fact that all 4.5 + billion of us human beings make a single species. In Pauline terms, it kicks against God's goading us to become one Body without distinctions of male and female, Jew and Greek, slave and free. Until our membership in the one Body becomes more important than our lesser, more derivative identities, we will continue to dishonor Jesus' passionate prayer (John 17) that we be one.

I think these thoughts about holism in the wake of the commemorations of the 500th birthday of Martin Luther. Participating in a local commemoration, a dialogue between Roman Catholics and Missouri Synod Lutherans, I was reminded again of the stiff-neckedness that afflicts all the Christian denominations.[8] Many Catholics don't live by the *kata holos* (concern with the whole) that gave them their name, and many Protestants continue to love a destructive, splintering independence. Even our small local panel quickly found itself back in the sixteenth century, pitting quotations from Trent against quotations from Luther. Lady Wisdom weeps over these blindnesses, these infantile refusals to grow.

PRESENCE

As we shall see in the chapters to come, the way to the holism of Lady Wisdom is an ongoing growth, a self-transcendence that keeps us ever reaching out, striving toward the whole. We are under way, on pilgrimage, if our spirituality is either contemporary or traditional in the best sense of these adjectives. We are becoming, in process, trying in our bodies to make up what is wanting to the sufferings of Christ. This does not mean, however, that we must be strangers to the earth or our fellow human beings, suspicious in the Gnostic sense. The wisdoms of Lady Hokhma are not separatist, esoteric, or elitist. How could they be, if the hallmark of the Lady's wisdom is its wholeness and the priority it gives to love? No, the feminist spirituality I am brooding anoints women's traditional inclinations toward family life, relationship, in short, the bonds woven at the dinner table. The wisdom of the catholic, universal Christian tradition is sacramental, taking presence in sex and kids, food and talk, the extraordinary variety of ordinary neighborhood living.

In her annotations on this theme of presence, Haughton uses the diary and life of a Belgian worker-priest, Egide van Broeckhoven.[9] Like the Little Brothers and Little Sisters of Jesus, the members of the religious groups inspired by Charles de Foucauld, Broeckhoven was content to work alongside ordinary people in a factory, share a cup of coffee and a cigarette in a tiny kitchen, and simply be a friend and fellow-sufferer of the indignities, the injustices, of our current economic classism. He was injured as any factory laborer might be, received typically cut-rate medical treatment at the company dispensary, and lost his life at age thirty-four when a load of huge steel plates slipped and crushed him.

Broeckhoven's diary reveals that he was passionately convinced that proclaiming the gospel today means identifying with the people to whom one is preaching. If the proclamation comes from the outside, it will seem a condescension of the privileged to the marginal and so will have little effect. It must come as Jesus brought it, as a presence to, a being in the midst of, the people to whom one is preaching, a living their life and dying their death. The modes of such an incarnational proclamation, not surprisingly, are the indirect and holistic modes of wisdom. One does not declaim from a pulpit but pitch in—to help another people hoist an especially heavy load, drain an especially bitter cup, celebrate a time of special gladness. The Body of Christ can easily be missionary and proclamatory in these ways, and always has been. Discerning pastoral theologians have always known that the grace that heals and elevates flows at lunch breaks, kaffee klatsches, times of neighborhood solidarity as much as in darkened confessionals or Sunday sermons. It is true that people often can't hear what we are saying because what we are shouts so loud. It is true that Christ is what we eat, how we sing, whether we support and forgive. In his foolishness, God has chosen to take shape, become present, through our daily exchanges.

I reflect, then, on the presences that move in and out of a typical contemporary woman's day. Take the woman we have already seen, the divorcee who one day received notice through the mail that her marriage had been annulled. I shall fictionalize her day somewhat, to make it agree with the day of everywoman, the collective person I meet in class each semester, but I doubt that I shall falsify it.

The woman is confident now, as she was not at the time of the divorce, because for five years she has been making her way in the business world, and with increasing success. Now she directs part of a testing service, and her job involves traveling to set up employee testing for a wide range of industrial companies. In this business life she often meets the presence of money, which regularly directs the show. She meets the presence of power, both the formal kind that goes with an upper-echelon title and the informal kind that comes from jockeying for advantage, winning psychological games. Sex is an on-and-off presence, as the vagaries of climacteric men make them now forward and now withdrawn. Loneliness is a frequent presence, for at night, when the kids have gone to bed, the house seems empty, rattling, depressing. A few friends bring understanding, support, and good cheer, but they are not so effective as they were seven or eight years ago. She misses an explicitly religious dimension, the presence of a Christian community. That went when the leader of her parish left the priest-hood to get married and the community divided over how to deal with him and its new situation.

So the best I see, from the woefully inadequate viewpoint of an outsider, is a few modest acts of kindness, a pale presence of the Christ who pitched his tent next door to all of us. No Egide van Broeckhoven works alongside this woman as an explicit but largely symbolic minister of the gospel. No small conventicle of Christian friends helps her meet Jesus in the breaking of the bread and have her heart burn within her. I am distant, more than 1500 miles away, but I doubt that I would make a crucial difference. I have miles to go before I will be able to make the wisdom and love of Christ present the way I ought. My exchanges are still clogged with sin and doubt, self-concern and hesitancy.

POVERTY

When Haughton comes to summarize the changes that a generous response to the passionate God would bring, she focuses on pov-erty. What the Lady Wisdom sees, the wholeness she seeks, is often best understood by those who are not prospering. The vision in-spired by the passionate God calls for a direct, unpersnickety re-sponse, which is more liable to come from people at the margins of a society than from people at the centers of money and power.

Doris Lessing, whose *Canopus in Argos: Archives* may be read as a series of reports from Lady Wisdom on the necessities to which we must bow if we are to survive in the future, uses women at sev-eral points as examples of people whose poverty has made them unusually free to see and act. In the scenes that precede the fol-lowing description, Klorathy, the narrator, has come as an agent of Canopus (Sirius), charged with trying to help the inhabitants of Volyenadna, who have been suffering from food shortages. Klor-athy gets nowhere with the men, such as Calder, who represent the several wretched little political groups that are vying for power on Volyenadna. The woman who has been waiting on table as he has talked, to no avail, with Calder about new foods that would set the planet free of its greatest constraints is the one who responds. Instinctively, she knows that it is not rhetoric that will improve her situation but direct action. Her contrast with the stupid politician, whose clevernesses conspire to prevent him from seeing what is in front of his face, is devastating: "And he got up, conscious of a hundred pairs of eyes for whom his demeanour, enduring modestly heroic, was intended. Without looking at me, he shouted out: 'The Sirian gentleman will pay.' As the woman came in, he grinned at her, like a child who has won a point over another, made a grimace towards me that categorized me as a hopeless lunatic, slapped her across her large buttocks as a way of re-establishing his balance, and went out. The woman stood looking at me. Like all their females, she is a rock and a stone, all strength and ability to withstand. She came slowly across and stood by Calder's empty chair. The following is a full record of the conversation I had with this female of Volyenadna. 'You say there is this food?' 'Yes. I have spores of it here.' 'When I plant it, how do I look after it?' 'You don't. It will grow on any rock. Here is a list of the methods you can use for preparing it.' 'Thank you.'"[10]

In three sentences, this poor woman has moved into action. The comparatively well-off characters who populate the novel speak volumes and never get off the dime. Lessing is giving us lessons in the debilitating effects of contemporary political rhetoric, which she paints as a sort of mental disease, but she is also making a marked contrast between the ways of people who are truly up against it, for whom talk and action are not luxuries but matters of survival, and the fat cats who can afford to debate, distinguish, delay endlessly. The fact happens to be that in most societies the female population is more likely to be up against it, pushed to the wall, than the male. Thus it is the female population that is more likely to cut through the rhetorical smokescreens and act. When one's children are hungry, one will endure a great many insults, push through a great many obstacles, to get food. Klorathy must wish that most of his dealings were with poor waitresses like this woman, rather than with posturing politicians like Calder. Then the wretchedness of the land he has been sent to help might start to lessen. Certainly Jesus, on mission to alleviate an analogous wretchedness, found himself beatifying the have-nots, who alone had ears to hear his message.

In the debate about women's sins that will figure in chapter four, we shall see something of the controversy that recently has raged around pride. Women's sins, feminist theologians have been arguing, have tended to be weakness and debility, cowardice rather than pride. What these theologians do not always say, or say not as clearly as Haughton's and Lessing's reflections on poverty lead me to desire, is that any moral disease that blocks exchange is pernicious. A weakness or poverty unwilling to let itself be turned to active account would be no Christian or even human virtue. A poverty that simply ground people down and took away their heart should be cursed and damned. But a poverty of spirit (often rooted in material deprivation) that showed in a leanness, a readiness for action would always be a blessing. Unless feminist religion gets it clear that this sort of poverty is good and desirable, a sign of Lady Wisdom's presence and solicitation, it will have missed something centrally important.

The goal of feminine wisdom cannot be establishing both genders at the center of a prosperity and power that corrupt. Simply to have more female senators and bishops, when the senate and bishopric are self-satisfied and pharisaic, would be no progress. For Haughton the poverty that will hasten the Kingdom is an identification with the poor Christ who was sovereignly free, an identification with the poor masses who know the corruption of riches and power. The good life that Lady Wisdom holds out, the goal of the vision that powers my feminist spirituality of self-transcendence, is the common life that comes into view when spirits that are stripped, lean, and free conspire to make learning and healing the center of culture, love and creativity the pearls of great price. It is easier for a camel to pass through the eye of a needle than for a rich person to enter this common life.

3   *ON SELF–TRANSCENDENCE*

Having introduced the context of the feminist spirituality I seek, and then hinted at the vision it can achieve in such poetic servants of Lady Wisdom as Rosemary Haughton, I would like now to start defining this spiritual vision, using work of the contemporary theological community. Specifically, in this chapter I will use the ideas of what might be called the new transcendentalist school: Bernard Lonergan, Eric Voegelin, and Karl Rahner. Then I will introduce the ideas of other contemporary thinkers that complement these central notions. The results, I hope, will be a solid foundation for Lady Wisdom's vision, a clear support from some of the most able thinkers on the contemporary Christian scene.

Bernard Lonergan's membership among the most influential of contemporary Christian theologians is well established. His works have inspired a school with such outstanding members as David Tracy, Matthew Lamb, and Fred Lawrence, and every likelihood is that Lonerganism will continue to thrive well into the twenty-first century. The beginning of Lonerganism, for all but the earliest aficionados, was the book *Insight*,[1] which focused on the act that gives it its name: the flash of light in which we grasp what something is, how a group of data fits together, where the solution to a problem lies. Archimedes running from the bath in excitement, sure that he has solved the problem put to him by the king, is the great example of insight.

For Aristotle, insight was the first of two key acts of the mind, and it answered the question, "What is it?" The second act (judgment) put together or kept apart the subject and predicate of a proposition ("The crown is [is not] made of pure gold"). Thomas Aquinas upped the existential and theological ante, stressing the attribution (or denial) of existence (*esse*) that goes on in judgment and making the act of insight the prime analogue to the procession of the Son from the Father in the blinding mental life of the Trinity.

Lonergan brought this tradition into the twentieth century by rethinking it in scientific and personalist terms. Insight is the act from which scientists derive their hypotheses. Judgment is the fruit of the process by which scientists verify or falsify their hypotheses. In both of these mental acts, as in the act of decision which follows upon judgment, the personal knower makes a commitment. The commitment to the hypothetical yield of insight is significant—even before he had tested his hypothesis Archimedes loved it for the light, for the release of tension, and the new vistas of implication it had brought. The commitment to judgment is more significant still, which is why few of us complain that we have poor judgment, while many of us complain that we have poor memory. And in decision we put our whole selves on the line, saying that we will (or will not) move into action. For Lonergan the progression from experience (the precondition of insight) to insight, from insight to judgment, and from judgment to decision is a steady march of greater and greater self-transcendence. With each step we stretch ourselves, knowing more and risking more. With each step reality changes for us (usually by growing bigger and richer), and we change with it, for in these acts of transcendence, of going-beyond, we see that we and reality are isomorphic: we are patterned to one another.

Because he thought in this dynamic, self-transcending way, Aquinas described the fulfillment of the human being as a beatific vision in which one would constantly be understanding, having a deepening insight into, the whatness that explains the whole of creation: the essence of God. Because he wanted to move Aquinas' genius into the contemporary world, Lonergan shifted from the metaphysical categories of the medieval world and spoke of "intentionality analysis." Were we to do a careful phenomenology of how people actually know and love, Lonergan proposed, we would find this dynamic, ongoing, self-transcending process to be at the very center of "being human." Then, taking this central dynamism as our Archimedian lever, we would be able to map the world that is proper to human intelligence, grasp the inevitably open-ended character of history, and solve the troublesome problems that have afflicted modern philosophy, which has oscillated between idealism and empiricism like a yo-yo in the hands of a child.

The Lonerganian solution is a critical realism, based on a profound analysis of both insight and judgment. While insight is the glamour girl, all glitter and light, judgment is the more important operation, and its reflective, self-analyzing character brings out the kinship between the cognitive side of wisdom (knowing the build of reality) and the affective side (loving realistically, in face of the divine Mystery). The way up to these signal human achievements is the way down to the depths of judgment, for judgment is the act in which we know what we can know, why we can say yes or no. Like the intuitive, poetic balance of Haughton's vision, Lonergan's critical realism is a winning blend of both an empiricist's concern for hard data and an idealist's awareness of the creative powers of the mind. It makes the knower a remarkable event and makes the development of human knowing into wisdom a matter of the most significant self-transcendence.

RELIGION

The self-transcendence that moves us from experience, through understanding (insight) and judgment to decision (loving), is an intentionality that implicitly carries with it the question of God. What makes the whole of experience intelligible? Is there anything whose existence is unconditioned, self-sufficient? Why should we struggle to decide for true values rather than false, embrace things good in themselves and benefitting the commonweal rather than things simply gratifying to ourselves? Insofar as we probe these underpinnings of our intentionality, we run into the question of God. In the master's own words: "The question of God, then, lies within man's horizon. Man's transcendental subjectivity is mutilated or abolished, unless he is stretching forth towards the intelligible, the unconditioned, the good of value. The reach, not of his attainment, but of his intending is unrestricted. There lies within his horizon a region for the divine, a shrine for ultimate holiness. It cannot be ignored. The atheist may pronounce it empty. The agnostic may urge that he finds his investigation has been inconclusive. The contemporary humanist will refuse to allow the question to arise. But their negations presuppose the spark in our clod, our native orientation to the divine."[2]

Our native orientation to the divine is sustained and illumined by the Holy Spirit, God's grace—Lonergan would quickly add that. But it is so native that we may see it at work in all sorts of people to whom the Holy Spirit would be a puzzle, or maybe even cause for invective: *anathema sit*! "Never mind such missing of the point," the Lonerganist will say. "Look not at what people say but at how people actually think, ponder, commit themselves or hold back. They do not do these things without assuming that the world is thinkable, that judgment intends what is real, that it is worthwhile trying to choose what is worthwhile. In a word, they do not do these things without becoming engaged with what, were they to extricate it and speak about it plainly, would be the question of God."

I have long liked this bent of Lonergan's for what people do rather than what they say. It squares well with the advice that Einstein gave those wanting to understand science: Concentrate on what scientists do, not on what scientists say about what they do. Equally, it accords well with the advice that Newman (one of Lonergan's mentors) gave to both his fellow-preachers and the flocks to whom he preached: Aim at things (and the words will follow). So when I find people who are intelligent, and who spend themselves in the service of intelligence, working long hours in laboratories or libraries, I mark them down as people who, were they to go to the grounds and implications of their service, would find themselves asking about the intelligibility of working their intelligence—the grounds for their having placed on insight such a large bet. The same with people who take pains to judge well, be fair, parse all the data one more time, root out their prejudices, and combat their skepticism: They are people whose pains make little sense if there is no foundation to truth, no reality that is unconditioned, not dependent on some other frail entity. It is the same with people who strive to be good, to choose and love well.

But is the presence of God only implicit? Are we condemned to the pale comfort that our drift into, or our vigorous pursuit of, self-transcendence *may* imply a Light, Being, and Goodness without measure? No, not everything is merely implicit. We can run into explicit, vivid comforts. The most fulfilling of these, for Lonergan, come through religious experience: "As the question of God is implicit in all our questioning, so being in love with God is the basic fulfillment of our conscious intentionality. That fulfillment brings a deep-set joy that can remain despite humiliation, failure, privation, pain, betrayal, desertion. That fulfillment brings a radical peace, the peace that the world cannot give. That fulfillment bears fruit in a love of one's neighbor that strives mightily to bring about the kingdom of God on this earth. On the other hand, the absence of that fulfillment opens the way to the trivialization of human life in the pursuit of fun, to the harshness of human life arising from the ruthless exercise of power, to despair about human welfare springing from the conviction that the universe is absurd."[3]

Now, the love of God that fulfills human intentionality is something brought about by the Holy Spirit. The Spirit does usually give this gift to those who hunger for it—people questing to understand, engage what is real, become honest and loving. But the gift itself is a free flooding of the heart that marks one as a child of God. When it comes, the whole intentionality process pivots and knowledge no longer calls the tunes. Henceforth, love is the leader, a love that would purify knowledge of its oversights, arrogances, self-servings. To the theme of self-transcendence the love of God adds the final climax: one reaches out in unrestricted fashion, trying to become equal to the Light and Goodness that found the world, spread through the world, solicit admiration and benevolence everywhere they are exchanged. So the saint, the person deeply in love with God, is a universalist, as students of religious development regularly find.[4] At home in the world that God has make, the saint sees it whole, loves all its parts, and learns that this love is the light of wisdom, the Lady's secret. A God's-eye view is a vision of love. It can discriminate and point out defects, but it cannot stop loving and nurturing what is good.

NOESIS

In Lonergan's dynamic view of human consciousness I have found a powerful endorsement for spirituality-as-intelligent-growth. The person who apprentices herself to this master soon realizes that becoming whole, advancing in wisdom, is a matter of always being willing to move beyond, following the Spirit's allurements. Whether through science, art, theology, prayer, or any of the many varieties of practical service, one finds a steady pressure to understand more widely and deeply, judge more soberly and fairly, decide more generously, further open one's heart to a love that would be unrestricted, enamored of goodness wherever found. Eric Voegelin's writings tend to the same conclusion, but with more attention to the history of human consciousness. For Voegelin the order of history, the intelligibility we can discern, best emerges when we study the history of order: how the various civilizations and epochs have spoken to themselves about the constitution, the organization, of reality.

Prior to the axial age 2500 years ago, when seers as diverse as the Hebrew Prophets, Zoroaster, Plato, the Buddha, and Confucius addressed human awareness, *homo sapiens* was a cosmological being, overwhelmed by the significance of nature. The main symbolisms of order at this stage of consciousness group together under the rubric of what Voegelin calls "the cosmological myth." The basic notion behind the cosmological myth is the aliveness and completeness of the cosmos. Characteristically, pre-axial peoples think of the world as an organism, a sort of democracy of participants who range from rocks to human beings. All the participants bear one another a certain kinship, for all are manifestations of the same potentially sacred, revelatory "stuff" that constitutes the cosmos as a whole. Thus there is a "consubstantiality" that links human beings to brother bear, father sky, mother moon, sister waters. Brother bear can "speak" to human beings, signify potently in human consciousness, because he is more like human beings than unlike.[5]

In Voegelin's reading of history, such spiritual strivings as those expressed in the Hindu Upanishads, the Buddhist Sutras, and the writings attributed to Confucius and Lao-tzu show a break with the cosmological myth. They all show an appreciation of the new organization of reality that becomes possible when one appropriates human distinctiveness. So, for example, although it remains true that the Tao courses through all of nature, playing the tunes that sway the ten thousand things, it is in human society that the Tao gains a voice, an articulate awareness. Thus it is in human rituals that the cosmos is solemnly appreciated and reverenced, to the benefit of human society and natural processes alike. Confucians tended to stress the human side of this symbiosis, Taoists the naturalist side, but both were aware of a new anthropocentricity.

On the other hand, none of these Eastern advances broke decisively with the cosmological myth. In all of the classical Eastern societies nature remained a living, somewhat personified milieu. So, especially in the folk strata, the consubstantiality or "same-stuffness" of all natural things continued to feed astrological, totemic, and roughly shamanic tendencies to venerate or try to appease naturalistic forces, spirits, and energies. The traditional Chinese *feng-shui* (geomancy), for example, has influenced architecture, landscaping, town planning and the like down to the present day. Only in two places, both of which pushed the Western civilizations to break with the cosmological myth, did anthropocentrism become the almost ruthless controller. These two were Greek philosophy and Israelite revelation.

The key finding of Greek philosophy, which reached fullest vigor in Plato and Aristotle, was that human consciousness is a light with a metaxic ("in-between") character. It stretches from the unbounded (*apeiron*) of primal matter to the One (ordering principle or *Nous*) that gives the world order. The golden mean is a life lived in consonance with this insight, a life that stretches upward toward the One but never forgets its roots in primal matter. At the richest moments in the history of Greek philosophy reason is itself clarified as a movement, a *zetesis*, that takes the form of a knowing ignorance, an unease with one's present confusions, that turns out to be the drawing (*helkein*) of divinity itself. Thus fully human life takes the form of a pursuit of the ground of existence, the foundation of reality.

Voegelin's own language describing this view of human life is difficult, but one cannot read it carefully and not see the self-transcending, dynamic character that it imparts to human spirituality:

Consciousness is the area of reality where the divine intellect (*nous*) moves the intellect of man (*nous*) to engage in the search of the ground. Aristotle has carefully analyzed the process in which the divine and the human intellect (*nous*) participate in one another. In his language, man finds himself first in a state of ignorance (*agnoia, amathia*) concerning the ground (*aition, arche*) of his existence. Man, however, could not know that he does not know, unless he experienced an existential unrest to escape from his ignorance (*pheugein ten agnoian*) and to search for knowledge (*episteme*) . . . The search, thus, is not blind; the questioning is knowing and the knowing is questioning. The desire to know what one knows to desire injects internal order into the search, for the questioning is directed toward an object of knowledge (*noeton*) that is recognizable as the object desired (*orekton*) once it is found . . . The search from the human side, it appears, presupposes the movement from the divine side: Without the *kinesis*, the attraction from the ground, there is no desire to know; without the desire to know, no questioning in confusion; without the questioning in confusion, no knowledge of ignorance. There would be no anxiety in the state of ignorance, unless anxiety were alive with man's knowledge of his existence from a ground that he is not himself.[6]

Implications abound, but the point I would underscore is the enormous religious potential latent in the unrest of those—my students in women's studies classes among them—who are searching for sense, order, a grounding for their lives. They are restless for an object or a goal that God is luring them toward: a grasp of the real divinity that is the final cause of both the world and themselves. One need not go apart from people's existential unrest, their pains and confusions, to find a realistic spirituality. When we have exegetes who show us the significance of our confusions, this spirituality is revealed to lie right in the striving to make order in our lives.

PNEUMA

The achievement of the classical Greeks was what Voegelin calls a "differentiation" of consciousness. From what had previously been an undifferentiated whole (cosmological consciousness),

Plato and Aristotle built on the work of their forebears and distinguished a precisely noetic component. They came to appreciate the structure of the human mind, and they were convinced that this structure applied wherever members of the human species thought, worked, pursued (however vaguely) the ground of their existence. Naming this noetic strand and clarifying the general structure of human intelligence was an epochal achievement. For Voegelin history demarcates itself and reveals its structure precisely through such achievements. They are breakthroughs, "leaps in being" that become points of no return. As long as people continue to think in the train of the epochal achievers, they cannot go back to a pre-epochal state of awareness. And so it has been, first in the West and then in the entire world. Despite the fact that the classical Greeks' achievement was blurred in Hellenism, and has suffered other forms of derailment, Western consciousness—science, political theory, philosophy, religion—would have taken a far different path without it.

The same is true of the second great leap in being that Voegelin distinguishes, the breakthrough of Israelite revelation. This, too, was an epochal differentiation, a point of no return. Even more than the Greek clarification of noesis, Israelite revelation broke with the cosmological myth. By symbolizing beyond any doubt a God who transcends the world, who is not immanent but beyond and independent, Israelite revelation created a revolution in human consciousness. With Abraham, or whoever actually received the experience of a God independent of the natural world, history brought forward another new thing.

The difference between the two differentiations, the Greek and the Israelite, is the difference between mind (*nous*) and spirit (*pneuma*). Voegelin has compared Paul—as heir of the Israelite prophets who clarified the revelations of the transcendent God—and Aristotle on this point, bringing out the different ways they express an equivalent understanding of human existence:

> The symbols are equivalent, but the dynamics of existential truth has shifted from the human search to the divine gift (*charisma*), from man's ascent toward God through the tension of Eros to God's descent toward man through the tension of Agape. The Pauline *pneuma* is, after all, not the philosopher's *nous* but the rendering

in Greek of the Israelite *ruach* [spirit] of God. Hence, Paul does not concentrate on the structure of reality that becomes luminous through the noetic theophany [revelation of God], as the philosophers do, but on the divine irruption which constitutes the new existential consciousness, without drawing too clear a line between the visionary center of the irruption and the translation of the experience into structural insight. Paul distinguishes between *pneuma* and *nous* when the order of the community compels him to do so, as in the case of the tongue-speakers, but he does not expand this effort into a philosopher's noetic understanding of reality; the dividing line will remain rather blurred as, for instance, in I Corinthians 2:16, with its quotation from Isaiah 40:13, where the *ruach* of Yahweh is rendered as the *nous* of the Lord, preparatory to the assurance that we, for our part, "have the *nous* of Christ." The theophanic event, one may say, has for Paul its center of luminosity at the point of pneumatic irruption; and the direction in which he prefers to look from this center is toward transfigured reality rather than toward existence in the cosmos.[7]

Several points here can be extricated and turned to our account. First, revelation stresses the divine gift it experiences its truths to be. In other places Voegelin has noted that the philosophers, too, spoke of their visions as free happenings, matters of grace, so that we should not make hard and fast distinctions between philosophers and prophets. Nonetheless, it is the initiative of the love of God rather than the anxious questing of the human seeker that captivates the prophet's interest. Even though the quest of the human seeker turns out to have been stimulated and supported by God, in the experience of revelation the action of God is much more overt and unavoidable. It is as though God's spirit or breath (*ruach*) breaks (irrupts) into a human situation or personality, giving it a new center of awareness, a new point for viewing. Paul is so overwhelmed by this new center of awareness that he does not bother to work out all of its correlations with other faculties or strata of consciousness. The theophany that riveted him (the Christ event) means a new transfigured reality. After all, God has resurrected Jesus—a completely unheard of thing—and thereby revealed a zone of glory, an inward reaching of heavenly power previously unknown. The first task is so to describe and communicate this irruption that people may grasp its world-shaking implications. It is a later task to think through how this irruption correlates with existence in the ordinary natural world (which of course continues).

By focusing on the spirit that the grace of God transforms, Paul has given us a second locus of self-transcendence. His imagery is not so dynamic as the Aristotelian imagery of questing. It is more passive and mystical. But its ultimate import is even more transforming than that of the Greek noetic insights. Through revelation God has taken the world up into the divine order of existence. If the philosophers discover a mind-to-mind connection between God and human beings, the recipients of revelation discover a spirit-to-spirit connection. In the movement of our spirits to love, for example, we can discern the drawing of God's spirit. In the still moments when we abide with a sense of the divine presence, the spirit of God is at work transforming us. This Pauline set of instincts will be crucially important when we come to the issue of Christian prayer. Because of the biblical tradition of pneumatic differentiation, we now can speak of a God who always remains other, beyond, but whose work in our prayer transforms us into what She herself is eternally.

MYSTERY

The third of our transcendental thinkers, Karl Rahner, has emphasized the pneumatic presence of divinity as an irreducible Mystery, a fullness of light and love that for our limited minds is bound to seem dark and will often appear empty. This means that "God," the reality we try to name with our received three-letter word, is sui generis, very different from the other realities with which we contend each day:

> The individual realities with which we are usually dealing in our lives always become clearly intelligible and comprehensible and manipulable because we can differentiate them from other things. There is no such way of knowing God. Because God is something quite different from any of the individual realities which appear within the realm of our experience or which are inferred from it, and because the knowledge of God has a quite definite and unique character and is not just an instance of knowledge in general, it is for these reasons very easy to overlook God. The concept "God" is not

a grasp of God by which a person masters the mystery, but it is letting oneself be grasped by the mystery which is present and yet ever distant. This mystery remains a mystery even though it reveals itself to man and thus continually grounds the possibility of man being a subject. There can then follow from this ground, of course, the so-called concept of God, explicit language about him, words and what we mean by them and try to say to ourselves reflexively, and certainly a person ought not to avoid the effort involved in this process of reflexive conceptualization. But in order to remain true, all metaphysical ontology about God must return again and again to its source, must return to the transcendental experience of our orientation towards the absolute mystery, and to the existentiell practice of accepting this orientation freely. This acceptance takes place in unconditional obedience to conscience, and in the open and trusting acceptance of the uncontrollable in one's own existence in moments of prayer and quiet silence.[8]

The pneumatic reality that irrupts into history through Israelite revelation and the Christ event is not like the things with which we ordinarily find ourselves dealing. We cannot easily differentiate God from the finite things we regularly experience, because God is neither finite nor a thing (a circumscribed entity). To know God one must participate in the movement that has brought God into the world as the ground of the reality the questing mind seeks or as the breath-like force that takes the human spirit where it has unknowingly longed to be. Since such a participation depends upon God as well as our own dispositions, our own alertness to a possible disclosure and hunger for it, we can overlook God and live as though there were nothing but finite entities, missing the subtle solicitation of the Spirit.

Moreover, there is no way that we can pin God down or mount up to God as a secure end to a chain of reasoning. We never master the Mystery, the totality of being that revelation shows is the constant presence of Creator to creation. The only way to know the real God is to give oneself over to the Mystery, to abide, watch, and pray. We can do this in formally religious ways, with considerable agony, knees sore from long hours on hard chapel floors, imaginations filled with gripping icons. Or we can do it almost casually, by letting ourselves enjoy the uncalculable splendor of a spring day or keeping ourselves present to sources of deep grief because we can lick our wounds in no other way. At such times we can experience that the "more" into which our joy takes us, or the void of our grief, is a constant objective feature of our spiritual horizon. The Mystery we somehow intuit as the most significant thing about us is always there whenever we avert to it, yet it is ever far from us and always exceeds our comprehension.

Rahner says this mystery may reveal itself to us, but that even in such revelation (for example, the experiences recorded in the Hebrew Bible and the Christ event) it remains a Mystery, a fullness we cannot fathom. We are who we are, receiving our subjectivity from the "call" of this Mystery, its allurement of us, but we never become its masters and always find ourselves its dependents (Muslims would say, its slaves). To be sure, we fashion words, images, and propositions about this mysterious God, so as not to be entirely helpless and be able to share our experience of it with others, but these words risk doing more harm than good if we detach them from the basic, originating experience of the Mystery itself. In the concrete order of human life as we actually struggle to live it (Rahner's "existentiell" order), the best posture is to accept the Mystery, open up to it, let it more and more become the religious (ultimate) horizon of our lives.

When we strip away external pressures and conventions, simplifying ourselves so that we listen in utter stillness to the voice of conscience, we sense the holiness of the Mystery, what it means for Rahner to say that the Mystery grounds the possibility of our being subjects, people called to respond. It is the ultimate norm or criterion of our lives. It is the same when we accept what is beyond our control and acknowledge the transhuman dimension to life, what earlier cultures called fate. This, too, can magnify the Mystery for us and break our lives free of the constrictions to which Madison Avenue would confine them. Like Lonergan, Rahner ends at an unrestricted view of human destiny. The climax of self-transcendence is the Mystery by which the eternal God is a constant presence in daily human history.

INCARNATION

For Rahner, the human person is a listener for a Word of revelation from the divine Mystery. Take human drives to know and love to their limit and you will place the human personality before the Mystery, open and expectant. In analyzing what the human being is "owed" by its Creator, Rahner—like most Catholic theologians —finds that revelation is not included. For the Creative Mystery to disclose itself as personal, loving, and forgiving is an utter gratuity. Yet Christianity stems precisely from this utter gratuity. Christianity is the religion that derives from Jesus of Nazareth, the Christ, whom his followers have long believed to be the Incarnate Word of God. The actual order of Rahner's theology has the Incarnation as the starting point, for Rahner never denies that his faith in Jesus Christ orients his analyses of the dynamics of human consciousness. He thinks that these analyses have an integrity and persuasiveness of their own, such that one need not believe in Jesus Christ to find them attractive, but he quite frankly admits that his faith has shaped his understanding of human nature through and through.

The center of Christian faith is Jesus, in whom God has spoken a once-and-for-all, irreversible, eschatological Word of grace and forgiveness. Where philosophic probings of the Mystery leave the prober uncertain of the status human beings have before God, theological probings in the aftermath of the Christ event can build on the New Testament's assertions that nothing can separate us from the love of God in Christ Jesus (Romans 8:39). Jesus therefore is the mercy of God, the divine compassion.[9] In his flesh the Christian finds the basic sacrament of the divine will to free human beings from their sinful bondage, love them out of their irrational closures and communicate to them the divine life. In terms of God's loving initiative, Jesus is an unthinkable condescension: In him the divine has emptied itself of its privileges and taken on our lowly human status, even suffered our human malice: "Have this mind among yourselves, which is yours in Christ Jesus, who, though he was in the form of God, did not count equality with God a thing to be grasped, but emptied himself, taking the form of a servant, being born in the likeness of men. And being found in human form he humbled himself and became obedient unto death, even death on a cross. Therefore God has highly exalted him and bestowed on him the name which is above every name, that at the name of Jesus every knee should bow, in heaven and on earth and under the earth, and every tongue confess that Jesus Christ is Lord, to the glory of God the Father" (Philippians 2:6–11).

In terms of his human achievement, Jesus is the revelation of what we images of God can become when we do wait upon the Mystery and take its revelations to heart. For Rahner Jesus is the perfect exemplar of a potentiality that all human beings share, insofar as their spiritual dynamics open them to the Mystery. We are the peculiar creatures who, without in any way having the divine life owed to us, can be elevated by God so that we become sharers in the divine nature, subjects of what Eastern Christianity has called *theosis*: divinization. Rahner somewhat breaks with the typical Western stress on soteriology (the logic of salvation), which has made the Incarnation mainly God's way of saving fallen humanity from sin. He doesn't deny this at all, but the Eastern theme of divinization seems to him of equal importance. The two themes converge in the iconic Christ whose "emptying" reveals the paradoxical form that the divine life tends to take within history. When Haughton speaks of the passionate God, she means much more than God's ardor to unite himself to human beings like a romantic lover. The divine love is a suffering, self-spending love (*agape*).

More than Rahner but in line with his thought, Haughton works out the implications of the idea that Jesus' followers now compose with him one Body. The extension or ongoingness of the Incarnation is the flesh of those who bear the passionate divine love like a stream within the flood of evolutionary history. When Christian believers let their imaginations feed on biblical imagery, they can sense that after Christ all human culture takes on overtones of passion and resurrection and somewhat reenacts the emptying of the Incarnate Word. Certainly for Paul the resurrection made possible Jesus' gathering of his followers to himself in a new way, incorporating them as members of his freed body. Loosed of the limits of mortal life, Jesus could associate with his followers in degrees of intimacy previously impossible.

None of this sort of probing, in the nature of the case, can be very exact. All of it remains but a glimpse of what God has intended through the resurrection. Yet all of it suggests that the Incarnation is now our human affair as much as God's historical affair. The Body of Christ in which the saving Mystery now reveals itself is the lovely flesh of the servant saints, the torn flesh of the poor and persecuted. Wherever the Spirit uses human openness, even human brokenness, to infiltrate love, make new beginnings, and combat infections of the heart, the incarnation of the Word gains another nuance, another quantum of helical progress. The flesh of Jesus therefore is the exact hinge of Rahner's profound understanding of grace. Divinity gives itself irrevocably in the body of Jesus, who lives now as the resurrected Christ, the head of many members.

FORGIVENESS

For a spirituality of self-transcendence, Jesus represents an iconic ideal. The self-giving love through which he revealed the most intimate nature of God made him a new paradigm of human perfection. As Lonergan has emphasized, love takes over the initiative in the order of grace. Under the guidance of the Spirit of love, Jesus was willing and able to love to the extremity of his death on the cross. When Christians make the cross the focal point of their faith, they should make sure that Christ's love, rather than his sufferings, is their cause of wonder. Otherwise they can seem to be promoting a strange glorification of pain, a sadistic notion that God's ways are blood and gore. God's ways deal with blood and gore and have something overwhelming to say about all the sunderings that creation suffers. But God's ways in themselves are always ways of love, overtures to exchange, gracious efforts to heal human flesh and raise it into the divine community of Father, Son, and Spirit.

The Incarnation, then, should serve us as a startling model and concretion of the self-transcendence that God's Word made possible when it emptied itself and identified with our historical neediness. And among the prime components of our historical neediness forgiveness surely bulks large. When one surveys human history as a whole, what stand out are wars and conquests. Tribe after tribe bloodies its neighbor. As soon as the species reaches the level of civilization, it seems to feel a crazy imperative toward conquest. In smaller scale, most clan and family units throughout the 10,000 years or so of recorded history also reveal a strong need for forgiveness. Between men and women, youngsters and elders, enough hurt flows back and forth to make forgiveness a small-scale imperative. That Christians' main model of love should bear directly on forgiveness therefore makes Christianity historically acute. Bracketing for the moment questions about how effectively the church has mediated forgiveness through the past 2000 years, we can agree, I hope, that the ever-relevant example of Jesus' forgiving love is one of our species' most inexhaustible resources for historical progress.

For Christian faith, however, Jesus' forgiving love is more than just an example. It is a structural constant as well. If sin is a constant in every human landscape, so is grace, God's forgiving love. If Jesus is raised and the Spirit is blowing where She will, the powers of forgiveness, reconciliation, and new beginnings are at work up and down the face of the land. As soon as one takes a close look at a tangled situation of conflict, these powers become relevant to the point of razor sharpness.

Take, for instance, the case of marital partners who have become estranged. Because he is well aware of the biblical depiction of God as forgiving, a theologian such as Walter Kasper can highlight the resources for reconciliation that inhere in the Christian marital bond: "It should be clear from what we have said so far that the doctrine of the sacramental bond of marriage does not in any sense give a totally legal structure to marriage. On the contrary, the doctrine is an ontological expression of the lasting aspect of promise and grace contained in sacramental marriage. It points to the constant claim that the partners can make on each other and their openness to each other. It follows therefore that a husband and wife who are separated have a constant duty to forgive each other and an unquenchable hope of reconciliation. This duty and hope may perhaps go contrary to human experience. In faith, however, we may accept that God's love and faithfulness in Jesus Christ never cease, even if human love and faithfulness are broken."[10]

In explanation of this quotation I would note, first, that Kasper is here assuming the Catholic view that marriage is one of the seven major sacraments through which the Christian community mediates God's grace. This sacramental view of marriage goes much more to the heart of the matter than any purely legal structures (for example, the many prescriptions of canon law) ever can. The sacramental view, on the contrary, is something ontological —concerned with the inmost being of the relationship between the two spouses. The promise that God makes in any official vehicle of grace and the promise that the spouses make to one another is at the heart of marriage, as is the grace of God itself: it is the love-life toward which God is luring all those of alert mind and good heart. For Kasper the sacramentality of marriage implies that the partners have an ongoing claim upon each other. In marrying they pledge constant openness, availability, and mutual help. Sexual intercourse is the vivid symbol and enactment of such pervasive availability.

Second, coming to the painful situation in which the cream of human relationship has soured, Kasper argues that the claim of the spouses upon one another continues even when they have separated. They are impelled, by their history of sacramental commitment, to try to forgive one another and become reconciled. This may seem an heroic demand, but nothing else makes sense if we are looking at the spousal relationship in the light of what God has pledged (how God has married into human history) in Jesus Christ. And, of course, sometimes this forgiveness does happen. Sometimes people move themselves from even very bitter enmity to mutual forgiveness and significant reconciliation. They may not be able to take up their old common life, but they grow and transcend themselves enough to stop being enemies; they resume wishing one another well.

TACITNESS

We have reviewed some of the major doctrines of the Christian worldview, as they have recently been explained by leading theologians and philosophers. In these final reflections on transcendence I wish to add a few grace notes. My hope is they will bridge the way from the rather masculine layout of self-transcendent faith that has dominated big-name theology lately to the feminine views that we shall consider in the next chapter. The first grace note, concerning tacitness, comes from Michael Polanyi, the distinguished philosopher who stresses the personal quality at the center of all knowledge.

In Polanyi's depiction of the rise of human awareness through the evolutionary process, tacitness plays a major part. There is always much more knowledge in us than we can articulate. The part of the world that we hold in clear relief is but the tip of the iceberg. Thus we communicate, understand, and give back meaning with much more than our words or other formal symbols. Communication can be grateful for human language, but it rests on a foundation of what Polanyi calls "conviviality": shared life and common roots in the same strata of experiences, both present and (genetically) past.

Women have won a deserved reputation for skill in many indirect forms of human communication. Through their intense, even symbiotic connection with children, and their emotional acuity, women have tended to develop a wealth of para-denotative ways of knowing and expressing. We do these ways a great disservice when we lump them together as "intuition" or "feeling," and then deprecate them as less significant than reason. The tacit and whole is the mother of the express and partial. The iceberg is more impressive when we see the bulk lying under the water.

Speaking of how human beings come to agree in their judgments and so bring their communication to fruition, Polanyi sketches the wider implications of the conviviality and tacitness on which successful communication rests:

> The interpersonal coincidence of tacit judgments is primordially continuous with the mute interaction of powerful emotions. The sexual embrace wordlessly communicates an intense mutual satisfaction. Animals which rear their young establish between parent and offspring a mutual satisfaction, coloured by dominance and submission. A baby smiles back at a smiling adult and is frightened into crying by a frowning countenance, without any practical experience of their corresponding dispositions... Diffuse emotional conviviality merges imperceptibly into the transmission of specific experiences in the kind of physical sympathy which overcomes the onlooker at the sight of another's sharp suffering. One has specially to train oneself in order to stand the sight of a surgical operation. Even experienced doctors may faint or get sick at the sight of a deep incision into the eye of a patient. Sadism is the transmutation of transmitted pangs into pleasurable excitement; it is a masochistic sharing of another man's torment and is known to be associated with masochism in the subject. Even the most determined criminals are liable to be affected by physical compassion. It is on record that when the head of the Gestapo, Himmler, desiring to test the tech-

niques of extermination at first hand, ordered the killing of a hundred Jews in his presence, he came near to fainting at the sight. In spite of deliberate training to merciless cruelty, upheld by a firm conviction of its rightness,the horrible sight of their deeds proved a serious difficulty to the persons charged with mass exterminations and it was in order to reduce this "seelische Belastung," that the gas chamber was eventually adopted.[11]

First, Polanyi here reminds us that tacit judgments—by which we agree sufficiently on how the world is structured to get along socially—run in tandem with an equally significant stream of shared primordial emotions. Second, these emotions produce a kind of physical sympathy when we observe someone suffering. Indeed, it takes special training (or perversion) to block this rise of sympathy in the presence of suffering. Third, even the Nazis recognized the "spiritual burden" that observing suffering could become, but instead of this leading them to recognize Jews as fellow human beings, as equals by the primitive verdict of instinctive emotion, it led them to further distance themselves from the evidence that they were going against everything natural and decent.

In introducing these reflections on how human connections are subtler and more basic than rationality, my concern is to stem any notion that "self-transcendence" diminishes our social solidarity. It is true that human knowing moves to break the bonds of muteness that afflict animals. It is false that the most sophisticated, adequate models of human knowing and developing demand a separation of self from all the tacit connectives that an embodied intelligence inherits. Let Polanyi's conviviality and tacitness, then, stand as background for our stress in the next chapter on women's inclination toward relationship and care. For, not only are these ways of communicating and so modes of growth, they are also ways to keep our rootage in the earth, the tribe, the common weal. Set in the context of our communication with the Spirit, and in the context of our communication as members of Christ's Body, tacitness and conviviality, like relationship and care, name the ways that a great deal—perhaps a majority—of faith's "business" is transacted. The priority of grace then comes to include the wonder that God has made us people who find it hard to choose isolation and closure.

MYTH

The relation between myth and reasoned theory parallels the relation between what is tacit and expressed. Myth is deep and pervasive, the underside of our iceberg. It is the storied way that we talk to ourselves about our place in a mysterious world, our convivial connections with nature and other people. Where reason tries to distinguish and clarify, myth evokes the splendor of the whole. Where reason is limited to what can be verified, myth bounds off in unfettered imaginative flights. Because of its ties to our psychic depths and imagination, myth helps to preserve our spiritual lives whole and palpable. Were doctrine the only form of religion, we would shrink to half our potential. Myth helps us to realize our full potential by taking us into sacred storytelling, holy play. There are more things in the world than are dreamed by clear doctrine. Myth is an ambassador from the world of dreams, a defense against doctrinal aridity.

In our programs of self-transcendence, we should go gently with the old myths of our childhood and show some kindness toward the new myths of our own time. Take the old story of Adam and Eve, the myth lying at the very head of the Book. To this day, Adam and Eve keep before us the wonderful beginnings of our human family, which are forever lost to strict reason. There is no way that we can recover, in terms a critical historian would approve, the origins of our human tribe. What it was like for the first animals who came to reflective consciousness must ever be a conjecture, a piece of fantasy. In the conjectures of the authors of Genesis, however, we have a treasured sense of how the sort of God revealed to Abraham, active in the Exodus, "must" have dealt with creation and the first human beings. He must have made the world in gladness, rejoicing that it looked so good. He must have wanted his first images to prosper, to be fitted to one another and bear rich increase. The fall of this couple away from God into the divided world we all now know must have represented a failure of communication, in all likelihood a free breaking of exchange. Yet even this decline from the simple, effortless ideal has come to serve God's good uses. Clothing Adam and Eve, God sees them out of the garden, makes them start to take responsibility for their knowledge of good and evil.

One could write a similar reflection about the myth of Jesus, which stands on a different historical footing. Jesus was indeed a distinct historical person, subject to rational evaluation. But he was also a figure larger than life, a champion against all his followers' enemies. So he became the conquerer of Satan, the long-awaited Jewish messiah, the Son of man expected by Daniel, the second Adam conceived by Paul. These are poetic, storied, deeply creative efforts to render something of Jesus' mystery. They have become master paradigms for the Church, Jesus' people, whom they serve in round, allusive, holistic ways. Liturgically and devotionally, when people need a cause for joy or suffer *in extremis*, these images and the master-stories they guide bespeak the central Christian conviction: Christ has overcome the world. They comprise a sort of blank check, an empty form to be filled in as need arises. As such they are more useful than any absolutely denotative, specific confession of faith could be. This side of death we shall never know the particulars of the heaven that Jesus opens, or the extent of the hell he enables us to avoid. We shall never know the full power of "resurrection," any more than the full suffering of "crucifixion." But we can see enough in the allusions and images of the Christian story to tramp along well defended against our worst enemies. We can see why our ancestors in faith thought that if they clung to Jesus all would be well.

When we are open to the mythic side of our histories and psyches, we gain access to the full world of religion, the rich storehouse best explored by the saints. Then the saints become larger-than-life figures suggesting fourth and fifth dimensions to "ordinary" life. These fourth and fifth dimensions, in turn, help us transcend the safe, bourgeois worlds we erect and break out to the mysteries of real life. So a shrewd schoolteacher might from time to time introduce the saints and other things mythic, lest the pupils' narrownesses stunt their mental growth: "Ramsay was by way of being an authority on saints, and had written some books about them, though I have never seen them. You can imagine what an uncomfortable figure he could be in a school that admitted boys of every creed and kind but which was essentially devoted to a modernized version of a nineteenth century Protestant attitude toward life. And of course our parents were embarrassed by real concern about spiritual things and suspicious of anybody who treated the spirit

as an ever-present reality, as Ramsay did. He loved to make us uncomfortable intellectually and goad us on to find contradictions or
illogicalities in what he said. 'But logic is like cricket,' he would
warn, 'it is admirable so long as you are playing according to the
rules. But what happens to your game of cricket when somebody
suddenly decides to bowl with a football or bat with a hockey-stick?
Because that is what is continually happening in life.'"[12] Myth
helps us stay open to the unexpected aspects of life that reason on
its own is likely to miss. It helps us transcend our smug know-it-
allness and get down to the roots of being human, where the things
that may grow are well-nigh infinite, both in number and in kind.

LOSS AND GAIN

The last grace note that I want to introduce bears directly on our
images of self-transcendence. If we have an image of straight progress, nonstop linear advance, we shall soon run into a credibility
gap. Life does not advance in a straight line. Personalities do not
develop like railroad tracks, going straight from the present to
whatever death and judgment lie beyond the horizon. A better figure for growth, especially growth in the life of faith, is helical: an
upward spiral. The upward rise, which may be at a sharp angle
(for the brave and generous) or at a modest incline (for the rest of
us), justifies speaking of progress. Most of us do, with the years,
cut down on our stupidities and consolidate a modest bit of wisdom. The spiral provides for our sense of going over and over the
same things, again and again coming back to a place we have been
before yet each time finding everything somewhat different. If
these descriptions fit most people's experience, then transcendence
can flow with the seasons, work its will through somewhat pre-
dictable patterns of childhood, adolescence, adulthood, and old
age.

One of the more satisfying theories of personality development
on the crowded market today is Robert Kegan's *The Evolving
Self*, which uses a helical model. For Kegan, Piaget's theories of
how intelligence develops have broad implications for personality
growth as a whole. We are essentially beings with a hunger to
make meaning, and much of our sickness or health depends upon

our success or failure at this task. To prosper we must let go of old stages and work hard to consolidate new. It is somewhat like the child's struggles in its first year, when it must let go of the satisfactions of crawling (satisfactions only won by toil) if it is to pass on to walking.

For most readers of this book the two phases of personality development most relevant will be what Kegan calls the "institutional" and the "interindividual." The interindividual is the phase of maturity where one can balance separateness (a distinct personal identity) with inclusiveness (warm connection to other people). The institutional phase is a time of self-possession, when one lives within supportive forms (at work, in church, through ideologies) that keep the world well ordered. The institutional self can be ambitious, responsible, and hard-driving. Usually it finds it hard to be flexible, present to others, able to empathize without losing its own perspectives. What Kegan says about the culture that supports the institutional self, as well as that self's typical relationships, seems to me quite pregnant:

> The culture which holds, recognizes, and remembers the institutional balance is the culture of ideology. It takes its most obvious form in the domain of work but can (and usually does) operate just as powerfully in the construction of loving relations which get organized around the exercises and preservations of one or both parties; self-contained identity. Such relations can be mutually supportive, warm, loving; they might even be marital relations of long standing; what they cannot be is intimate. While the controversial, and possibly irritating, suggestion in Chapter 7 was that many of us who are chronologically adult are psychologically adolescent, the parallel suggestion in this chapter is that many adult relationships of closeness and affection (especially marriage) fail to be intimate. An understanding of why marriage is an increasingly perishable state (especially in an age when most of the nonpsychological reasons for remaining married have lost their potency) may depend on an understanding of intimacy that is not tied to cultural prejudice, a psychology of illness, or an arbitrary assortment of external behaviors ... but tied instead to the meaning of intimacy to the psychological present of an adult. I will return to this understanding, but for now the question to be asked of the culture which holds institutionality, the culture of ideology—whether it holds the person in the domains of love *or* work—is how available it is to pass its

charge over (or to evolve itself) into a culture which will support the post-ideological balance of interindividuality and intimacy.[13]

One of the most crucial times of growth, then, is when we must leave ideology, a framework that bolsters our independence by mapping the world very clearly, and enter the less chartable zones where intimate relations (those that give and accept revelations) occur. As Kegan makes plain, people can be close to one another physically, even have a marriage of long duration, without really being intimate or able to get beyond roles and guiding ideas to relate as the occasion demands. One must lose some of the (false) independence and surety of the institutional self if one is ever to gain full maturity: the ability to be oneself *in relation to* other free people, giving and receiving as an equal, deeply committed to the relationship by all sorts of bonds yet not drowned in it.

Certainly maturity should enable us to be both more ourselves, our individual personalities, and more intimate with others, more connected or included. Certainly the loss of independence that moving from the institutional phase requires is one of those "dyings" that the Bible makes the condition for true life. So certainly leaving a spurious surety and independence can be a genuine transcendence, a loss of the linear model to gain the helical model that rings much truer.

4

FEMINIST SHADINGS

K egan's work is interesting in itself, but interesting as well for the relation it bears to the work of Carol Gilligan. Both are students and fellow-workers of Lawrence Kohlberg, the psychologist who has most famously applied Piaget's ideas to moral development. Both have been sufficiently influenced by the women's movement to have recognized the disservice that models such as Kohlberg's, Erikson's, Freud's, and most other psychologists' have done by building their paradigms from almost exclusively male experience. In the regnant models of development, women's experience has been considered either deviant or irrelevant. Kegan has listened to the findings of researchers such as Gilligan, who have found women to have a different moral voice than men. His helical model, which swings back and forth between independence and inclusion, is in part an effort to provide for both sexes' experiences and integrate them into a fully human model of maturity.

I went to Gilligan's work after Kegan's, expecting it to be helpful but not anticipating how creative it would be in its own right. For the studies that Gilligan and her colleagues have done on women's personality development make it clear that women's typical patterns of crises and advances are quite different from those of men. These differences had long been obscured, because researchers applying models and tests such as Kohlberg's had simply scored women low when they did not produce the responses that male test groups had made normative. Only when people began suspecting that this was an anomaly, and then focused on the nearly complete

57

disregard of women's stories in the construction of the paradigms, did the door open to investigating women's patterns as possibly just as valid as men's.

At this point, I must make a brief excursus. *After* the fact of realizing that the dominant paradigms of personality development have been generated from an overwhelmingly male base of experience, it seems clear that they were *bound* to be skewed. However, unless we are to have this same painful experience in many other areas—suspecting dimly for some time that the ideal models don't fit the data but not knowing precisely why—we must clarify and then embrace an a priori principle such as the following: No model that does not factor in both sexes' experiences as equally important can claim general validity or merit loyalty. This would be true in legal, educational, religious, medical, and other areas. Until we have people represented in their appropriate sexual numbers (approximately half male and half female), we can't generalize about patterns or models of human experience. It seems an obvious principle, once one reflects upon it, but time after time I run into expectations, based on at least implicit models, that have been extrapolated from nearly exclusively male experience.

Returning to the specific matters of personality development and self-transcendence, I would note that the major deficiency in the received paradigms is their stress on logic, rights, and independence to the detriment of feelings, relationships, and connections. In a holistic model such as Kegan's, both of these lists of human qualities get their due. They are stereotypically male and female, however, and in paradigms such as Kohlberg's the second list stands inferior to the first, much less adquately provided for.

Stereotypically, when women are asked to solve moral problems, they place more emphasis on the second list of qualities. Men approach such problems by stressing the qualities of the first list. Men also have more trouble relating to other people satisfactorily and integrating emotion with reason than women do, while women have more trouble gaining independence, clarity of outlook, and self-confidence. Men have relatively little trouble gaining self-confidence, since the culture at large supports their self-assertion and our models of moral development place the independent, self-confident decision maker at the acme of maturity. So women suffer innumerable disadvantages in all the areas influenced by the paradigms, and the species as a whole is encouraged to wobble along one-sidedly. The secular gurus handle self-transcendence and spirituality just as badly as many religious gurus have.

THE DIFFERENT VOICE

In Gilligan's research, the female moral voice is distinguishable from the male as early as the eighth year, and by the eleventh year it is unmistakably different. For example, a typical eleven year old boy, answering Kohlberg's famous dilemma about Heinz, construes the dilemma as an opposition of rights. The dilemma is this: Heinz needs a drug if he is to save the life of his dying wife. He has no money and the druggist who possesses the drug will not give or loan it to him. Should Heinz steal the drug? An intelligent eleven year old boy usually will answer yes, Heinz should steal the drug, because the right of his wife to life is stronger than the right of the druggist to make a profit on his wares. A typical eleven year old girl, however, will not construe the dilemma in terms of opposing rights. (This immediately places her outside the Kohlbergian expectations.) Rather, she will approach it as a problem in human relationships, and she will seem uncomfortable with the limited choices the text has laid before her.

Consider, for example, the response of Amy, a bright eleven year old, when she is asked whether Heinz should steal the drug: "Well, I don't think so. I think there might be other ways besides stealing it, like if he could borrow the money or make a loan or something, but he really shouldn't steal the drug—but his wife shouldn't die either . . . If he stole the drug, he might save his wife then, but if he did, he might have to go to jail, and then his wife might get sicker again, and he couldn't get more of the drug, and it might not be good. So, they should really just talk it out and find some other way to get the money."[1] Other girls' responses tend to take a similar tack, avoiding a stark confrontation between legal rights and probing the possibilities of solving the problem by changing the relationships. So, for instance, many girls castigate the druggist for his inhumanity, pointing out that if he weren't insistent on his right to a profit, and saw more clearly the much higher value of a human life, the dilemma wouldn't arise.

That this more contextual and relational approach to a moral dilemma such as Heinz's places girls lower on Kohlberg's scale of moral development than boys, in effect penalizing them for their instinctive inability to think only in legal terms, is a small shame within the province of psychology. I would not minimize the implications of this shame, since ours is a narcissistic age, with millions overly interested in measuring how they are doing according to some chart of maturation. But the penalties that girls suffer by being scored lower in such research is by itself rather small beer. It is the unconscious bias of the test, and the relation of this bias to the biases of all the other tests, formal and informal, acknowledged and unconscious, on which our society relies that is the real problem. For if women do construe moral (and no doubt, other) conflicts differently than men, at least in our American society of the late twentieth century, and if this feminine construction is ignored by the paradigms that shape business, law, religion, education, and our other social institutions, then the injustice of the Kohlbergian gradings is repeated all across the land. In place after place, women are almost automatically being scored as less reasonable, decisive, less able to solve hard problems, and the like, because the regnant models have ignored them.

This reflection would be but a little exercise in logic, laying out the hypothetical inferences, were it not so apparent that the discriminating pattern is in fact a grim feature of real life. Certainly in all the institutional areas I mentioned—business, law, religion, education—men still control the flow of money and power, men still legislate and enforce most of the rules. It is true that women have become more prominent in business and law. It is true that women have, in some important statistical ways, long been preponderant in education and religion. It is not true that business or law shows any sign of turning to androgynous, helical, male-female paradigms in the near future. It is not true that education or religion runs by female models. Why? Mainly because men occupy most of the positions of power in all of these institutional areas, but partly also because women have assumed the regnant paradigms and so judge their own sex less astute at decision making (at least the formal, institutional kind) than the male.

So, women meet in other areas the same sort of injustice they suffer in the Kohlbergian tests. And, perhaps more ominous, other areas suffer the imbalance that affects recent developmental psychology. Business, for example, suffers from a lack of a "feminine" contextual sensitivity, a feminine creativity about relationships. Law is much less able to deal with subtle, contextual, and atmospheric matters than adequate justice would demand. Education has canonized scientifico-male models of knowing that have shortchanged the humanities, and are now crumbling before the newest physics. Religion has made sacred lore men's business (in Judaism, for example), or has denied women's competence to represent Christ (for example), in the Roman Catholic controversy about women's ordination to the priesthood).

In each case, the resources and needs of half the species have not factored into the decision making processes. In other areas, such as medicine and the military, the situation is quite parallel: small hearing is given voices calling for a holistic medicine; little appreciation shown for nonviolent ways of making peace and avoiding war. The grossness of this sexism is astounding when one steps back and ponders it whole. It is a remarkable measure of our sin and distance from Lady Wisdom. In fact, as racism was the great symbol of nineteenth-century American evil (and, of course, continues today), so sexism is the great symbol of our twentieth-century evil, although it may be more easily overcome, since this would serve the advantage of white women, who are potentially a quite powerful force.

RELATIONSHIP

Often the different psychological orientation of women expresses itself as a much stronger investment in relationships. On the whole, women seem considerably more concerned about keeping connections, ties to other individuals and groups, than men do. Much more than men, women typically define themselves not as isolated individuals but as group members, participants in such and such a family or work circle, swimmers in such and such a general stream. Their whole bulks larger than their individual parts. The maintenance of connection or relationship is so high a value that women will often subordinate to it many personal goals. For women, being is being-with, work is collaboration, a sense that we best decide by talking things through. So constructive building, rather than men's negative objecting or destroying, characterizes most women's group interactions. Therefore, dialogue and consultation tend to be more important than solitary brooding.

This is not to say, of course, that no women brood in solitude and no men consult. It is not to say that no women are destructive and no men can build. I am painting in broad strokes, combining Gilligan's descriptions of women's developmental orientations with my own observations of how women and men tend to behave. But I have no serious qualms about the broad characterization that has been emerging. From the popular stereotypes that one encounters in the mass media, to the refinements being brought forward by contemporary social science, the more relational pattern of women's ways of coming to understand and decide stands out again and again. For most women reality is markedly more ecological, symbiotic, relational, and processive than it is for men.

Now, my point is not to begin building a new philosophy of relationship or a new theology of connection, but to reveal some of the implications that women's relationality would seem to hold for an adequate model of self-transcendence, a spirituality likely to be viable for both sexes in the future. Recall the instinct of the eleven year old girl Amy to solve Heinz's dilemma by finding alternate ways to get the money, and so the drug. Amy does not conceive Heinz, his wife, or the druggist as isolated individuals. She sees them as ingredients in a holistic gestalt. Moreover, Amy quickly imagines further ramifications that the test problem itself barely hints: the possibility that Heinz will go to jail and so worsen things for his wife; the possibility of borrowing the money. Further, Amy is more concerned about the druggist than any simply legal rendering of the dilemma is able to be. She does not want Heinz to steal the drug, and one likely reason (in addition to her acceptance of our general proscription on stealing, and to the possibility that Heinz would be jailed) is the hurt that stealing would inflict on the druggist. As we shall see in the next section, *care* is a central ingredient in a distinctively feminine moral reasoning, and following closely on care is a strong desire not to inflict pain. Clearly, however, care also is based upon relationship, the fact that for women we are all in it together.

This sense that we are all in it together has, to date, kept feminism more an ally than a competitor of other liberation movements. Rarely, for instance, does a feminist pit women's rights or needs against those of peoples of color or other groups that are marginal to the centers of American prosperity and power. Part of this inclusiveness may stem from women's having been moved by the pathos in other underlings' sufferings. Another part, however, likely stems from women's aboriginal orientation toward the whole, the all of us, that make cooperation more natural than competition. It is not that women have a special virtue that helps them see unattractive people like the druggist in gilded terms. Some women may have such a special virtue, as may some men, but most women would not judge the druggist an attractive person. Rather, most women simply are less able than are most men to exclude the druggist from the moral calculus or make him simply the enemy. The situation is something whole, so the solution has to be something whole, a formula to which all of the participants have contributed. The same with the situations of real life, the social conflicts tearing apart real neighborhoods. The feminine instinct is to try to get all the parties talking, to try to bring all the sufferers some relief.

And where does this distinctive relationality or holism of women come from? One conjecture is that it comes from early childhood, which tends to be dominated by feminine role models and authority figures.[2] Whereas boys have to differentiate themselves from the women—mothers, teachers, baby-sitters—who dominate their early years, girls identify themselves with these figures. In most of the groups that girls will encounter in childhood, the authority and organizing focus will be female, and so it will call the girls to identify themselves with the whole organizational process. Boys will find most group situations more complicated, but frequently will have the feeling that their way to self-definition is by separation, distancing, focusing on their distinctiveness rather than their commonality.

I am not competent to judge the validity of this thesis, nor the validity of similar theses based on women's orientation toward childbearing and their consequent bodily sense of togetherness. For me, the fact that women do seem more relational than men is enough to raise a demand that the doings of the species as a whole honor this relationalism. Informally the species often does. Many, indeed, are the mothers and wives who receive plaudits. But such informality can do women in, making their contributions much less valued officially than men's, and much less recompensed. So too in spirituality. Until relationship becomes as honored a mode of growth as isolation, and group prayer and work become as potent vehicles of the spirit as solitary prayer and work, we won't have fully human paradigms for religious development.

CARE

From relationship comes care, a sense of responsibility for all the members of the gestalt. If the aetiology of care is somewhat murky, its potency is very clear. The prophet said that God could no more abandon Israel than a nursing mother abandon her child. For the prophet, a nursing mother was the *ne plus ultra* of loving concern, the example beyond which one could not go. Indeed, through history much of women's praise has devolved from their special caring. The beery songs that spell out M-O-T-H-E-R play on self-sacrificing care, as do many more estimable forms of laud. Women themselves tend to focus on caring, praising it in their female role models and expecting it of themselves. This is probably more helpful than harmful, especially in view of the needs of the species as a whole, but lately it has become obvious that care can be a great problem for women, a source of considerable frustration, retardation, and guilt.

For the care that society has praised has been the care that has redounded to society's direct profit. With "society" here being largely its male spokespersons, women have been praised for spending themselves at home for their spouse and children, taking on the volunteer work that makes our nobler institutions run, doing the cleaning and typing at the economically bottom rung of many work situations. Society therefore has been rather hypocritical in the praise it has lavished upon feminine caring. The 62-cent female dollar is inconceivable apart from such hypocrisy, as is the exclusion of feminine care from the boardrooms of power. As mentioned, none of the major institutions that one sees when surveying the cultural landscape has adopted androgynous, let alone feminist paradigms. The praise of feminine care that wafts through religion, education, medicine, or government is quite tainted, and more than vulnerable to the charge of being proffered in bad faith.

Still, women seem unwilling to give up caring, and their only caveat nowadays is that caring be extended to the feminine self. The daughters who look back in awe at their mothers' careful self-spending are starting to realize that often such spending was beyond measure, to the point that it gave away capital mother herself could ill afford to lose. Mothers overextended and under-rewarded tend to become mothers with axes to grind, grievances to parade, injustices to redress by fair means or foul. Easily do they weep, lament, manipulate, and drive others to teeth-grinding with their dizziness or incompetence. Had such women cared more for themselves, been less pressured by hypocritical models of care that lost sight of the self, they might have served everyone they encountered less ambiguously.

Relationships do not flourish when care is excessive, smothering, spending more of the carer's substance than it should. Care for the self should be like the love on which Jesus predicated his love of neighbor. We are to love our neighbor, he said, as we love ourselves. The fairest assumption, then, is that we are to love ourselves fully, with an eye to our own good, a strong striving for health and the development of our talents. If we are to be helpful we must be strong. If we are to be effective we must take the time to become competent, good and glad in our work.

Granted this, however, women still want to be caring. They still reject models of social existence in which individualism and competition threaten relationship. Although they have been going into the law in greater numbers, few women are completely happy with the law's adversarial structure, and many women only put up with the law's unattractive forms because working through them may prove helpful to their needy clients. The same with medicine and education. The women I see entering these professions are willing to try to take what is good in them, what these professions have grown to be under male auspices, but they are not willing to canonize what is impersonal or ruthless. Indeed, a large number of women in my field of education have a long agenda of reforms they are trying to push forward. Against the streams of power, they are trying to promote interdisciplinarity, consensual models of governance, humane support and evaluation of teaching, bias-free treatment of students (no more sexual harassment, for example), and other offshoots of an at least implicit rootage in care.

Since this discussion has a psychological context, I perhaps should add that Eriksonian care,[3] which becomes a main feature of generative adulthood, can in my opinion fit what women are struggling after quite well. The impulse to care may occur earlier for women than for men, and this may call for some redefinition of "adulthood," but in making it we might find ourselves mainly doing justice to girls' quicker maturation, which also seems left out of current developmental models. Eriksonian care clearly applies to parenting and work, and its general sense of bearing responsibility for the next generation would seem to apply to women in spades. If women typically must do more of their individuation or gaining of distinct identities through care than do men, this too could mainly shade the model, such that relationalism would get more attention. Care is so central in many women's own stories that I see no reason to cast it off simply because parts of Erikson's life-cycle scheme were formulated without reference to women's equal humanity.

WEAKNESS

The ambiguities in traditional feminine caring remind us that almost all human situations are a mixture of advantage and disadvantage, grace and sin. One of the merits of psychological approaches to tangled human situations is that they often help us to acknowledge such ambiguity, and reconcile ourselves to imperfections that are well-nigh unavoidable. This is true, for example, of Jungian analysis, which would have us embrace the shadow side of our personalities and realize that health involves some compromises with the devil. Theological approaches can learn something from this psychological sophistication. In a visionary such as Haughton one finds an acceptance of sinfulness, a consistent realism and compassion, but many other theological schemata have been rigid and absolutist. I think it should remain true, in Christian schemata, that God is light in whom there is no darkness at all (I John 1:5).

This need not mean, however, that God's images should aspire to a lightsomeness that would leave them pale. God's light is the spark in our cloud, as Lonergan put it, but we remain very earthy: imperfect, struggling, and a lot lower than the angels.

Some such compassion could bring care profitably to bear on the theological assessments of sin and soteriology. These, too, ought to have nuance, be patient and realistic. Feminist theologians have done us the large service of exposing male biases in traditional portrayals of sin,[4] but it remains a pressing task to get the feminists' whole discovery of women's underdevelopment into sharp focus. Moreover, although the traditional overly masculine model has focused pride as the capital sin, it has also left a full panoply of other vices, as well as a strong instinct that virtue is a mean, a graceful poise in the middle. The Luciferian image of *non serviam* has something to commend it, when one considers the carnage of a Hitler, Stalin, Mao, Idi Amin, Pol Pot, Ayatollah Khomeini, and whatever American butchers we might also nominate. Hurling their wills against heaven and the natural law, swelling their egos so that they blot out the light that keeps conscience human, these giant sinners have shown us what hellish existence would be like. Instructively, their pride almost always has had large admixtures of anger, envy, and other capital sins, but the root of the whole ugly disorder has been their refusal to exchange, commune, love. They have not seen Dante's love that moves the stars, and so they have not found Kant's moral law within. Their lack of love is their condemnation.

The typical pattern for women, as feminist analysts have been pointing out, is quite different. Women have on the whole been under-assertive, irresponsible, complicit with evil, fearful to the point of burying their heads in the sand. They have missed the mark, not gained the golden mean, by defect rather than excess, dispersion rather than conversion of love-energies into massive egotism or hate. In Dorothy Dinnerstein's terms,[5] women have become monstrous in the mode of the mermaid, the seductive siren, the spectator to history. Men have been minotaurs—brutal, mindless forces of lust and destruction. Women have been the mocking voice that has put some brackets around men's destructiveness, but they have not been effective psychotherapists, or fully courageous defenders of justice and peace. Whether or not one agrees with Dinnerstein's analysis of the main cause of this two-fold monstrosity (women's strong dominance of childrearing), her phenomenology is hard to pass by. She gets her reader's attention, and by the end of the book her anger at the "sexual malaise" that men and women have conspired to create seems a holy passion.

So, when women raise their voices against a care that would deplete them, a self-sacrifice that would render them impotent, they can enlist more than the many stories of individual tragedy. All too clearly, the glaring absence of one sex from human history has played a major part in the destructiveness of the species as a whole. "History" being, for Dinnerstein, the realm of decision making, production, and responsibility, women's exclusion from it (largely through men's agency, but with some female connivance) has been doubly dolorous. Not only have many women been kept adolescent, hand-wringing and wimpy, history as a whole has been kept adolescent, again and again suffering uncontrolled outbursts of aggression, imbalanced waves of feeling and vice.

However, I would not want my criticism of women's culpability for this to become a matter of blaming the victim. Nor would I want to ignore the many women in almost every age who have been splendid models of maturity, and without whose heroic labors things probably would have been much worse. At all levels of society, many "women of spirit"[6] have regularly brought forward a wholesome care that has valiantly combatted the worst monstrosities. That most male establishments have depreciated this contribution has only confirmed their waywardness, their blindness to the path that is straight. When women argue for new paradigms of sin and grace, therefore, they have most of history as their laboratory. The new grace that feminism should want, I think, is a care that is strong, fearless, and rightfully loving toward the self. It need not be strident or militant. It can go gently, like the Tao. But it will not back down or retreat from history, for it knows that future history is as much women's responsibility as men's.

TIMIDITY

The last facet of care I want to examine is the need women have developed to be cared for themselves. If, as Gilligan suggests, care/relationship is the distinctive feminine moral voice, what does it say for a feminist spirituality that the female stereotype has included the notion that women need to be cared for—supported, protected, and completed—by men? We may scoff at this stereotype today, and cite such neo-classic lines as, "a woman without a man is like a fish without a bicycle." But this *savoir-faire* is the fruit of a generation of intense liberation. The situation not many decades ago was very much as Barbara Pym, the great modern prober and satirist of British manners, portrayed it in *Excellent Women*: "Going back on the train Dora and I were both in an elegiac mood and started reminiscing. We no longer belittled our successful contemporaries or rejoiced over our unsuccessful ones. For after all, what had *we* done? We had not made particularly brilliant careers for ourselves, and, most important of all, we had neither of us married. That was really it. It was the ring on the left hand that people at the Old Girls' Reunion looked for. Often, in fact nearly always, it was an uninteresting ring, sometimes no more that the plain gold band or the very smallest and dimmest of diamonds. Perhaps the husband was also of this variety, but as he was not seen at this female gathering he could only be imagined, and somehow I do not think we ever imagined the husbands to be quite so uninteresting as they probably were."[7]

No doubt there were many reasons for past generations' fixation on women's marrying, but surely one was the need women felt to be cared for. In the larger world of business and supposed practicality, women were considered vulnerable innocents. They might be brilliant with children, the sick, or the elderly, but in "the real world" they needed a protector and provider. Those sighing with relief that such days of anxiety and heteronomy are long gone perhaps need to withhold some of their surety, for the abortion study Gilligan uses suggests that many women are still far from self-reliant.

The abortion study admittedly forcused on a somewhat unrepresentative group: largely college students and preprofessional women from the Boston area.[8] The idea was to interview women who were in the midst of real and difficult moral dilemmas, and study how they reasoned about and reached their decisions. What surprised me, however, was the great degree of confusion that characterized the abortion group. Granted the locale and character of the sampling, I had expected fairly well developed feminist notions about responsibility and choice. On occasion these notions came through, but stronger by far was the pregnant women's tumult. Several of them were considering their second or third abortion. Several more had taken no contraceptive precautions. A surprising number were being dominated in their decision making by husbands or boyfriends. A solid majority were pregnant from sexual relations with married men or boyfriends whom they knew were unsuitable prospects for fatherhood or marriage. True, a few of the subjects were teenagers, but most were women in their twenties. Again and again, they traced a pattern of stumbling into their binds, getting themselves into the situation because they were afraid to come to grips with what had been happening in their sexual relationships.

Of the twenty-nine women in the abortion study, twenty-one chose to abort. Four had the baby, two miscarried, and two could not be contacted to determine their final decision. Almost all the interviewees felt moral pangs about abortion. A few clearly thought it was a form of murder, and almost all considered it morally wrong. Several argued that they were in no position, economically or psychologically, to have a child at that time. Several more thought this was the time to take charge of their lives and assume responsibility for a decision that, however repugnant to their mothering instincts, seemed dictated by their circumstances. Without taking a position for or against abortion itself, Gilligan seems to applaud this move to decisiveness and responsibility. This is understandable, and the sort of sophistication mentioned previously would enable many of us to find and support the good features of even messy or downright evil situations.

Still, I wonder about the "responsibility" that suddenly came over quite a few of the subjects toward the end of their first trimester. Against the backdrop of their previous do-nothingness (and, for several, their previous abortions), it seems suspect. I wonder about the drift of the counseling that these women received, since so large a percentage of them chose to abort (21 out of the 25 clear-cut cases, or 84 percent). The reader finds little discussion of the option of having the baby and placing it up for adoption. By far the majority of the discussion swings between the options of keeping the baby and aborting it. No doubt my Roman

Catholic background is showing at this point, but I find so casual an overlooking of a *tertium quid*—an obvious way of preserving a potential human life while doing justice to the inability to raise a child well—a serious skewing of the dilemma. Certainly, the young women themselves were less to blame for this than were all the surrounding people, including especially the men who made the women pregnant, who failed to do their share. But even in their mitigated responsibility the women are sorry evidence that a great many females still live as though they expected others to care for them, that they still have not gotten down to the moral basics. It is fine to rejoice in their progress toward maturity through their abortion experiences, but I find it chilling that many counselors probably saw little tragedy in the 84 percent abortion rate that was the price of this maturation.

LANGUAGE

I have been trying to bring forward some of the shadings on self-transcendence, moral development, and the like that feminine care suggests. But I do not claim to have done more than introduce a rich and complicated topic. At this point, I would argue only that our models for spiritual development must take into account women's typically careful ways of conceiving their responsibilities (and so, much of their growth). The model I shall finally propose will blend the forward-moving self-transcendence that masculine analyses such as Lonergan's imply and the responsive, receptive, relational models that feminine analyses yield. Certainly, a masculine model such as Lonergan's has an important place for response—in religious development, for example, one largely follows the leadings of the Spirit. And equally certainly feminist models are encouraging movement toward women's proper self-promotion and growth. But the two need to be synthesized even better in Christian spirituality. They also need to be integrated with analyses of gain and loss (or, gain through loss) that might be especially helpful in difficult situations such as unwanted pregnancies.

Several other "shadings," however, clamor for attention before we get to a synthetic model. For example, there is the question of theological language. In the Christian doctrinal system, which of

course has a lot to say about Christian notions of spiritual development, patriarchal language has been the rule. Lately there have
been some cracks in the walls (even in biblical translations) regarding the generic "man," but in most denominations "God" still
is rendered with the masculine pronoun, and so is mainly thought
of as male. The roots of the problem of theological language, in
fact, come to rest at the conception of God: They lead to "theological" problems in the strictest sense. Until our notions of God
become as reflective of women's religious experience as men's,
and of women's imaginings of the divine as men's, the basic structure from which we work on our better spiritualities will betray
us.

Rosemary Radford Ruether is a major feminist theologian who
has addressed these theological problems in the strictest sense.
About sexism and God-language, she writes:

> Patriarchal theologies of "hope" or liberation affirm the God of
> Exodus, the God who uproots us from present historical systems
> and puts us on the road to new possibilities. But they typically do
> this in negation of God/ess as Matrix, as source and ground of our
> being. They make the fundamental mistake of identifying the
> ground of creation with the foundations of existing social systems.
> Being, matter, and nature become the ontocratic base for the evil
> system of what is. Liberation is liberation out of or against nature
> into spirit. The identification of matter, nature, and being with
> mother makes such patriarchal theology hostile to women as sym-
> bols of all that "drags us down" from freedom. The hostility of
> males to any symbol of God/ess as female is rooted in this identifi-
> cation of mother with the negation of liberated spirit. God/ess as
> Matrix is thought of as "static" immanence. A static, devouring,
> death-dealing matter is imaged, with horror, as extinguishing the
> free flight of transcendent consciousness. The dualism of nature
> and transcendence, matter and spirit as female against male is
> basic to male theology.
>
> Feminist theology must fundamentally reject this dualism of na-
> ture and spirit. It must reject both sides of the dualism: both the
> image of mother-matter-matrix as "static immanence" and as the
> ontological foundation of existing, oppressive social systems and
> also the concept of spirit and transcendence as rootless, antinat-
> ural, originating in an "other world" beyond the cosmos, ever re-
> pudiating and fleeing from nature, body, and the visible world.

Feminist theology needs to affirm the God of Exodus, of liberation and new being, but as rooted in the foundations of being rather than as its antithesis. The God/ess who is the foundation (at one and the same time) of our being and our new being embraces both the roots of the material substratum of our existence (matter) and also the endlessly new creative potential (spirit). The God/ess who is the foundation of our being-new does not lead us back to a stifled, dependent self or uproot us in a spirit-trip outside the earth. Rather it leads us to the converted center, the harmonization of self and body, self and other, self and world. It is the *Shalom* of our being.[9]

Ruether is certainly a liberation theologian, concerned to make her reflection on God bear good news to the oppressed, but she finds a deep flaw in the predominantly male liberation theologies that have been in vogue. In essence they neglect or in fear shy away from the feminine side of divinity or ultimate reality, which she names the God/ess. Their vision tends to be dualistic, pitting matter and nature against spirit and freedom (and associating women with matter and nature). The feminist theology that Ruether is developing tries to create concepts, and therefore language, that will overcome these false dualisms. It is in search of a divinity that will be the Shalom, the peace of our beings, that will bring us into the freedom, connection, and perfection for which we yearn. The God/ess who represents the ground-level sources of being would help us correlate our matter and spirit, our individualism and sociability. Clearly the patriarchal God has not done the full job, so perhaps the time of the God/ess has come. In the new, rooted, and natural transcendence, a God/ess who would bless women and men alike might usher in a going-beyond that would be fully caring.

JUSTICE

When feminist theologians such as Rosemary Ruether ask for a new theology that would do right by women's experience, they are simply seeking justice. Justice has been a capital notion in biblical theology, as well as in male liberation theology, so developments such as Ruether's simply hoist sexist liberationists on their own petard. We shall see more of this when we come to church politics, where women's essential (and very telling) tactic has been simply to quote the church's own ideals and compare them with the church leaders' sexist practices. Here, however, we may profitably pause to consider, first, the justice that feminist Christian theologians have inherited from Jewish and Christian sources and, second, the modifications that feminine experience is suggesting.

When Jewish ethicians reflect on justice, they are likely to claim a special priority in its promotion: "It has been widely stated that justice is the moral value which singularly characterizes Judaism both conceptually and historically. Historically, the Jewish search for justice begins with biblical statements like 'Justice (Heb. *zedek*), justice shall ye pursue' (Deut. 16:20). On the conceptual side, justice holds a central place in the Jewish world view, and many other basic Jewish concepts revolve around the notion of justice."[10] Christianity almost always does well to remind itself that Jesus was thoroughly a Jew, completely a child of the covenant that gave rise to such stress on justice. God has never repudiated that covenant, and whatever rightful variations Christianity has played on the notions of justice in the Hebrew Bible, whatever rightful differences Christian doctrine has sponsored in contrast to Jewish Talmud, a great similarity and debt remain.

Male liberation theologians have been quick to see the affinities between the biblical justice championed by the Israelite prophets and the best aspirations of modern social thought. Thus José Miranda has made a great deal of the convergencies between the biblical prophets and Karl Marx, finding in their common passion for justice a bond that makes them brothers.[11] Other prominent male liberation theologians, in both Latin America (Gutierrez, Sobrino, Bonino, Segundo) and North America (Brown, Coleman, Baum, Cone), have similarly laid great stress on social justice.

To render all people their due is at the center of the biblical heritage. This rendering is not antagonistic to mercy, love, and grace. It is ingrained in the concept of a God who frees people from oppressions that grind them down and deprive them of even the minima that are their due. If Jesus was a passionate defender of the poor, and a passionate foe of laws that got in the way of justice to the poor, he was no opponent of social structures that would institutionalize just economic, political, religious and other

arrangements. We have suffered too long a prejudicial interpretation of the Pharisaic movement that would immediately oppose
all striving for exactitude in developing justice, glorifying instead
an often amorphous evangelical freedom. When the military dic-
tatorships of Latin America and the economic steamrollers of
North America have submitted themselves to elementary rules of
fair dealing, there will be plenty of time to contemplate supere-
rogatory works of special mercy and charity. First let justice roll
down like a mighty stream. Then we can consider sophisticated
mystical relinquishments, poverties that are brutal on the body
because of special spirits' special needs.

These are theses that I find in the mainstream of male liberation
theology, and they apply to women with exceptional vigor, because
everywhere women are a majority of the poor and powerless. Nonetheless, the male liberation theologies—Latin American, Black,
and White alike—have been slow to recognize their myopia regarding women, their vagueness about the gender of their greatest
constituency. Recently this has started to change, but only because
women—Latin American, Black, and White—have kept prod-
ding the eloquent spokesmen to practice what they preach. However, feminist liberation theologians have also been extending the
concept of justice, making it more holistic or inclusive than it tends
to be in the mainstream of male Christian liberation thought. This
is not so much because feminist theologians have been foraging for
new data (although in some cases, such as the materials on Goddess religions, they have[12]), as because feminist theologians have
been developing a new paradigm of "justice."

The main thing that strikes me about this new paradigm is its
concern for the losers in history's battles. For example, feminists
are looking anew at the fertility religions of the ancient Near East,
which the biblical prophets severely castigated. Without giving
them carte blanche approval, several feminists have shown how
much was positive and healthy in these ancient views of nature,
sex, and women. Indeed, much in those religions was a healthy
counterbalance to Israelite patriarchalism and later Christian un-
easiness about the body. For a second example, feminist revision-
ists are showing that the Gnostics, who were losers in the early
Christian controversies that hammered out "orthodoxy," were
also people of insight. They had their faults, such as a distrust of

matter, but they were positively inclined toward both feminine wisdom and democracy.[13] Analogous cases could be made for the native traditions—African, Asian, Amerindian—that the Christian missionaries tended to deprecate. As feminist theologians have been wielding it, "justice" has become both broad and detailed. It has thereby become a concept eminently suited to the multivocal exchanges today's global pluralism demands.

COMMUNITY

When people strive to transcend their current oppressions and overcome their present unfairnesses, they channel spiritual growth into political health. In fact, we can have no authentic spiritual growth without contributing to political health. None of us is an island unwashed by or not contributing to the larger human and natural whole. Justice therefore orients us toward community, the togetherness we all have in virtue of our all being in "it" similarly. Women have been discussing community with special interest in recent years, and sometimes this special interest has drawn criticism. When they have spoken of bonding, going out of their way to connect with other women, some critics have found them uncatholic, separatist. Indeed, women who spontaneously identify with other women often find themselves accused of reverse sexism. This is a serious charge, and I find it only compounded when it occurs in the context of ecclesiology, our efforts to think through how the Body of Christ ought to appear.

Responding to this charge, Elisabeth Schüssler Fiorenza, a distinguished New Testament scholar, has made a point of some importance:

> The second objection made is the charge of "reverse sexism" and the appeal to "mutuality with men" whenever we gather together as the *ekklesia* of women in Her name. However, such an objection does not face sufficiently the issue of patriarchal oppression and power. It looks too quickly for easy grace, having paid lip service to the structural sin of sexism. Do we call it "reverse imperialism" if the poor of South and Central America gather together as a people? Or do we call it "reverse colonialism" whenever Africans or Asians gather together as a people? We do not do so because we

know too well that the coming together of those exploited does not spell the oppression of the rich or that the oppressed are gaining power over white men and Western nations, but that it means the political bonding of oppressed people in their struggle for economic and cultural survival. Why then do men feel threatened by the bonding of women in our struggle for liberation? Why then can churchmen not understand and accept that Christian women gather together for the sake of our spiritual survival as Christians and women persons? It is not over and against men that we gather together but in order to become *ekklesia* before God, deciding matters affecting our own spiritual welfare and struggle. Because the spiritual colonialization of women by men has entailed our internalization of the male as divine, men have to relinquish their spiritual and religious control over women as well as over the church as the people of God, if mutuality should become a real possibility.[14]

The quotation relies on the need women today feel to gather with their own kind and sense what it would be like to belong to a community that did not systematically, automatically, relegate them to second-rate status (for example, in terms of their power to symbolize the divine or lead the religious polity). Each women's group is a datum, a bit of evidence, documenting this need. But when Christian women gather, a special opprobrium, no doubt rooted in a special unease, often spurts forth at them, even from the mouths of otherwise liberal (seldom truly radical) Christians. The ideal image of a completely open church, with no divisive groups, rises up to block out the reality of the present church in which women are systematically divided off as the second sex. Perhaps the numerical majority of women gives rise to this fear and opprobrium, although in terms of numbers the recently colonized peoples also represent a fraction of the world population that approaches a majority. Or perhaps the objectors have yet to acknowledge the reality of spiritual deprivations and oppressions and can only see suffering in material terms. That would be a peculiar retardedness to find in religious people, but the world is indeed full of wonders. The fact is that women are a long way from threatening to become the ecclesiastical oppressors of men. We are still at the stage of trying to consolidate the elements of a spirituality of survival. Next might come the ways and means to share power with men as full equals in the Body of Christ. Only on the far side of that presently rather distant achievement would one be able sensibly to speak of a danger of female oppressiveness.

No, the problem is really a quirk in the male psyche, which again and again causes it to over-react. It is the uppity woman syndrome, still long-playing although recorded perhaps a century ago. Worse, it is sibling to the over-reactions of the colonists when the colonized began to gather together and pressure for their natural rights. For example (as the film *Gandhi* brought before the eyes of millions), when the Indian colonized began to gather together and pressure the British for their natural rights (as the indigenous peoples of the land), the British lost their vaunted coolness and civility, lashing out with brutal violence. Blood ran in the streets, because the British psyche could not abide the accusations in the Indians' simple demands. When the quirk in a psyche is really guilt, and that guilt is not acknowledged, violence can easily surge forward. Supposedly it is defending a form of "justice." Acutally it is keeping the violent from having to deal with their own sinfulness.

Most of the conflicts women presently have with their churches are spiritual, so the analysis of violence and guilt will be analogously spiritual. I find it largely to apply, however, in such cases as Pope John Paul II's efforts to get the American Catholic bishops to suppress the support of women's rights to ordination. This effort seems to me to fly in the face of the Catholic church's own teachings about public opinion, the charismata of the laity, the competencies and rights of all the people of God, etc. By its very unmeasuredness, it suggests a guilty conscience, a deliberate refusal to see the sinfulness of the church's sexism, because after such seeing things would have to change. Change would mean a loss of power, the kind of loss that many conversions entail. To gain the community that Jesus must have foreseen, if Jesus was not sexist, the Pope would have to lose ways of thinking and acting (ways perhaps far more ethnic in origin than religious) that he now enjoys. Realistically, that would be quite a good bargain. For so small a loss as the stony countenance and will that he showed Sister Teresa Kane when, during his visit to the United States, she broached the issue of women's ordination, John Paul II could gain legions of sympathetic sisters, daughters, and mothers, fellow-workers eager to join him in dialogue.

MINISTRY

Confrontations such as that between John Paul II and Teresa Kane would be comic were they not repeated analogously in so many situations and the source of so much pain. When a church founded to minister to people in pain, organized around a message of grace and liberation, itself becomes an instrument of pain, the play being enacted is a tragedy. The same criteria that feminists are applying to biblical sexism apply to such ecclesiastical tragedies: they cannot be the work or will of (any credible) God. No credible God wants to oppress, denigrate, or deny women their equal humanity. And just as it will not do to spin fancy distinctions about different kinds of "equality" so as to try to "save" the Bible from the charge of androcentrism (taking a nearly exclusively male point of view), so it will not do to try to excuse the church, the community of Christ, by semantic distinctions. The brute reality of the biblical literature is that it nearly always is androcentric or patriarchal: written from the viewpoint of male power-holders who do not grant women's equality in humanity and divinity (*theosis*). The brute reality of Christian church life today is similar: women's experience is not admitted on an equal footing with men's. The link between the two brutal realities is the dependence of current Christian church life upon the patriarchal biblical literature (and the centuries of tradition it begot).

This does not mean, however, that feminists should jettison the literature and past that begot their present situations. No, as Schüssler Fiorenza argues well, they should rather reclaim them. For such a reclamation would keep alive the memory of past women's sufferings from the Christian patriarchy and within the Christian community. It would also make today's women aware that many early Christian women were equal power holders with men. Indeed, at many points in Christian history, both during New Testament times and later, women shared in the leadership power of the gospel, shaped their community in the Spirit, and ministered the healing love of Jesus. Marginal though they tended to be to the official flow charts of power, they sometimes got recognition as the de facto leaders of the community. At such times motifs of several New Testament communities reappeared, for early on "the Jesus movement" was an egalitarian stream opposed to the "love

patriarchalism" that finally came to dominate.[15] In a careful re-
trieval of their history Christian women will therefore find many
solid achievements, hopeful precedents, and complications to
simpleminded readings of downtroddenness. Often the women
who preceded us in faith have been the vessels of amazing grace.
Therefore amazing grace (and hard work) just could usher us into
a very good tomorrow.

Combining the egalitarian facets of early Christian ministerial
love with contemporary feminist sensibilities, I see at least the
adumbration of a ministry that would have a central place for a
purified and empowered feminine care. And, in such a foreshad-
owing, it becomes almost embarrassingly clear that right now
many women are doing the things of a new Christian ministry, a
new Christian priesthood, in all their depth, sacramentality, and
variation. As Haughton suggests, right now Lady Wisdom is moving many people, individuals and groups alike, to bring forth the
love of Christ in new ways that threaten the inauthentic traditions. Right now, women's special aptitudes for including all members of a group, settling differences, and bringing a gentle touch of
concern are making the good news of freedom, salvation, and new
beginnings palpable in thousands of places. Sometimes this takes
the humble form of apparently ordinary teaching, nursing, or
mothering. Other times it takes the form of ceremonial leadership,
as women's rituals give a new face to old and precious enactments.
This bread broken by women's hands and shared around a table is
an old communication of Christ filled with new overtones. Wine
blessed and drunk in common is the old mixture of pain and joy,
but tasting new because of new circumstances and new psychoso-
matic needs.

Still thinking about the synthetic paradigm I want to fashion,
the helical blend of pushing ahead and caring, I find myself imagining that most Christian ministry has approached to the mode of
care, whenever it has had in it the mind that was in Christ Jesus.
The power and authority of Christ Jesus showed themselves in service. Emptying himself of anything grand, let alone arrogant and
isolated, Jesus learned God's designs for him, grew in wisdom and
grace, by more and more identifying his good, and God's will,
with the care of other people. So it was natural for him to tell
Simon Peter, as John 21 sets things up after the resurrection, "feed

my lambs ... tend my sheep ... feed my sheep." Putting aside our contemporary reluctance to cast any people as "sheep," we cannot miss the Johannine intuition. Love of Christ shows in a careful nurture of those about whom Christ is concerned, those whom Christ considers his flock. All the care that women have generated through the centuries, and all the care that women are trying to clarify today, bears directly on the work through which Christ learned and revealed God's will, the work for which Christ gathered his disciples.

So the tragicomedy of Christian women's ministerial situation in churches like the Roman Catholic and Eastern Orthodox moves another turn of the screw. Women are denied the service in which many of them see the joyous possibility of finding themselves as Christ found himself, because they lack a physical identifiability as Christ-the-prime-minister-of-the-sacraments; yet what the official, institutional Church denies or temporizes about, the actual people of God are manifestly pushing forward. The actual current ministries of women, rich and varied, show that feminist spirituality is already transcending many old road blocks, is already a full spiral beyond what the patriarchal is able to conceive.

INTERLUDE

FREEDOM

I have introduced the notion and contemporary setting of a feminist spirituality conceived as self-transcendence, anticipated many of its features by sketching a vision enlightened by Lady Wisdom, worked through some of the major findings of recent transcendentalist thinkers (male), and reflected on the shadings that recent feminist theology and developmental psychology place on such major findings. In my view, this has all been background: clearing the land, assembling the machinery, getting the sets in place. The foreground-to-come is the concrete areas—prayer, work, family life, politics—where women struggle to live out whatever notion of spirituality they have generated. Between background and foreground, act one and act two, comes this interlude, where I want to consolidate the probings of the first part by molding the model that will serve us in part two. If I were to put this to myself in terms of a single pointed question, it would be something like this: Would you please make as sharp as possible what you mean by the self-transcendence that could serve women well as their spiritual focus, in what they are trying to achieve in their struggle after personal religious growth?

The two general words that I would use to characterize such self-transcendence are freedom and love. Freedom carries much of the load that the onward-pushing, over-going motifs of the male transcendentalists assemble. In Lonergan's model the person is free to experience, understand, judge, decide (love), and following out this freedom (this call of human nature to grow) will increase it. Indeed, it will bring the person to the point of an unrestricted love, an opening of mind, heart, soul and strength that tries to match itself to the unboundedness of the divine Mystery. The free person therefore is on the move, under way, convinced that her inbuilt drives to know what is real and embrace it in love are a beautiful birthright, an imperative from the muses of authenticity. No heteronomous, outside agency can rightly contradict this drive, because to contradict it is to oppose the way that God has constructed the human personality. We are made ever to question, ponder, and try to achieve what is good. Realism and goodness are the inalienable goals or achievements for which the spark in our clod burns. Any institution or foreign body that does not share these goals, or that tries to prevent us from pursuing these goals, is inauthentic. As inauthentic, it cannot be a work or servant of God. The old Platonic criterion remains completely valid today: Something is not good because people say that it is "godly" (revealed, inspired, traditional). Something is godly because it is good (consonant with light, productive of welfare).

On the whole, men have been quick to claim a birthright of freedom. Hormones and history have conspired to make men barely think twice before striding forth to claim their destinies. Their hubris, excess, and lack of regard for others show the bridles to which freedom must submit, if it is not to become a wild stallion, useless and dangerous. But there is something deeply human about the conviction that we are made to grow, learn, develop. We ought constantly to be like Montessori kids, aflame with curiosity and wonder. Even when experience shows us the melancholy, dark side of experience, we ought to count this part of the adventure, welcome it with a wan or wry smile. Time is our milieu, our condition. Unless we are moving through time forcefully yet gracefully, dancing all the measures as they unfold, seeing all the movements as contributing to a whole, we are missing our meaning. T.S. Eliot saw that many people have the experience but miss the meaning. In freedom we must probe for the meaning and then move forward toward the next experience that beckons.

So my model does have the cutting edge of an upward spiral, the knife of a helix that pushes ahead. We women ought to chant to ourselves, as a sort of mantra or power song, that it is for freedom that Christ has set us free (Galatians 5:1). We have every bit as much right to grow, work our minds and refine our hearts, as men. The call to love God with whole mind, heart, soul, and strength is as much ours as any man's. When Jesus enjoined his listeners to be perfect (Matthew 5:48), he did not exempt women. Today such a perfection breaks the bonds of *Kinder, Kuche, und Kirche*. It is at least as broad and deep as women now find growth and care to entail. Unless Christianity can embrace this breadth and depth, it will fall below the best of contemporary secular idealism. What a mockery that would make of Christ's perfection, the love he poured out unto the end! What a fraud it would expose the church to have become! The future is women's as much as men's. The right to shape it and the responsibility to bear it are encoded in our chromosomes as deeply as in men's. So our spiritualities have to set our faces before history in deep-breathing freedom. We have to fill our lungs, quicken our adrenalin, get ourselves in shape. If this means more willfulness, more self-concern, more ambition, more drive—so be it. Our God is not a god of the dead but the Mother of the living.

First, then, there is the affirmation of freedom: day and night, for country mouse and city mouse, in every climate and color of skin. We are all called, enjoined to come alive and grow. What opposes this call is evil, sinful, diabolic. Political regimes, economic regimes, religious regimes, educational regimes that deny it or render it impossible are ripe for revolution. Feminist spirituality as self-transcendence means fighting for the truth God has called us to discover and incarnate, laying down life for the friends God has commanded we give justice. We can only be God's when we are free. We can only imitate Christ by considering the lilies of the field, the birds of the air, the way Christ cared not a damn for the good opinion of blind guides.

LOVE

Freedom alone, however, is not the holistic spirituality I find women to covet. The feminist spirituality I see aborning would synthesize freedom with love. And "love," of course, is just as grand a term as freedom, capable of just as many interpretations and abuses. I shall mean several things by it, but in the first place "a positive care." Love is the animating spirit behind healthy relating, tactful nurturing, self-spending that is not masochistic but admirably generous. It can be strong as death, as the Song of Songs knows. It can be bereft as crucifixion. The Pauline hymn to love in I Corinthians 13 is a good bit of Christian phenomenology. The reflections in I John bring out love's kinship with God's life and the soul of a religious community. The passionate romantic love that Haughton applies to God comes from the singular literature of medieval Provençal. The much older Confucian notion of *jen* and Hindu notion of *bhakti* pitch in with helpful similitudes from the East. We are what we love, even more than what we eat. We are what we want to love, for where our treasure is, there will our heart be. And so it goes, this playing with "love," gilding of "love," that theologians can no more avoid than poets. Without love we are nothing: tinkling brass and clanging cymbal. Without love we do not do justice to women's historic grandeur, women's contemporary spiritual needs.

So, my model has love, and I find it to soften the crudeness and hurt that unbridled freedom can bring. I find it to make the helix more graceful, more like the good witches' spiral dance,[1] less like a metallic screw. When love is synthesized with freedom it does not veto pushing ahead, striving to grow. Erotic love is very much like freedom's striving. Its pursuit of beauty, personal fulfillment, the world that might be is, in fact, the self's most energetic, delight-filled pushing ahead. On the other hand, love does have chastenings in store for freedom, purifications that freedom may not initially want. At the heart of the religious matter, converse with God is a dialogue, and in a dialogue one listens as well as speaks, is receptive as well as productive. There would be no honest dialogue with the Christian God, Father or Mother, if the human partner came with a rigid list of non-negotiables. The Bible, like any sacred book, is the judge of its reader, as well as a collection of texts today's reader has critically to sift. Love enables us to bear the judgment of God that comes through scripture, tradition, and the example of the saints. The same Spirit who insinuates God's love-life of agape is occasionally Mother enough to brood our need to die so that we may rise to fuller life. She is like a refining fire, a living flame, that would burn away any sin keeping us in bondage, any fetter on our self-transcendence.

I realize that this is rather traditional language and that it has often been abused. But I see no way around it. Unless we are to separate ourselves from prior female Christian exemplars, who have blazed with the gospel's passion for what is right, we shall have to contend with sin, purification of the self, the ways of God that are as far above as the heavens are above the earth.[2] If we care about God, we care about God's ways and try to make ourselves disponible to them in the Spirit. If we care about other people we listen to what they tell us they need, how they perceive God's will for them, even if this demands that we shift away from egocentricity and abrade our selfishness. To say that in the past women were brought up to worry overmuch about selfishness is not to say that even healthy women do not continue to be selfish. Discerning what is healthy self-love and what is unhealthy takes no little spiritual maturity (and so no little fasting, watching, and praying). The question we should ask about any language or practice is not whether it is traditional but whether it serves well today, in a time of raised feminist consciousness. Opinions will differ about particular practices, but I myself would doubt a wicca who made no place for conversion, asceticism, the love that makes loss the condition of many gains.

Nor is this all. There is also the matter of loving our enemies, doing good to those who persecute us—Jesus' most harrowing command. Qualifications are in order, of course, and justice does not fly out the door. But Christian love is inseparable from forgiveness, reconciliation, and pledges to make new starts. I think that Mary Daly is right to write herself out of the Christian camp, for she seems unwilling to accept this central doctrine.[3] Her spirituality becomes, as Schüssler Fiorenza sees, something for a coven of outsiders, a group that wants no truck with either oppressive men or incompletely liberated women.[4] The several chapters she writes on the injuries that women in several cultures have suffered from men makes Daly's position understandable, but they also give her care a splenetic tone. As a result, her humors are dark and gnashing, like old furies nursing grim grievances. Like Schüssler Fiorenza, I want no cheap grace that would erase the evils of past history without repentance and reparation. But I also want no future that stands under a dark cloud of militant hatred and has no place for shafts of forgiveness and new starts. Where would any of us be without forgiveness? How could any spirituality make progress? We all have sinned and fallen short of God's glory. We all need to be freed by her careful love, which looks more to what we want to be than to what we are or ever have been.

5   *PRAYER*

NATURALNESS

I have sketched a model of feminist spirituality as self-transcendence. It is a helix whose two sides are freedom and love, masculine pressing ahead and feminine care. The model tries to provide for drive, intelligence, and expansion toward the infinite horizon of God. It tries to provide for relationship, exchange, eros, agape. It is an imperfect model, simplistic and vague, like all models that presume to capture the heart of the religious matter. Nonetheless, it is my little model, my child, so I shall defend it fiercely. To detractors on the right who want no uppity women, I shall lay down women's utter equality with men in the right to develop, grow, and serve in full human freedom. To detractors on the left who want no talk of love, softness, care, suffering, or forgiveness, I shall lay down the utter basis of Christian and all religious wisdom: we react more than initiate, suffer more than control, and discover our real selves more as creatures than creators.

In the chapters to come I will rethink the major zones that my feminist students worry about in terms of this helical model. The first such zone is prayer. Traditionally, prayer is the lifting up of mind and heart to God. Today it may be the settling of mind and heart down to God, but the import is much the same. Prayer is our formal exchange, deliberate acknowledgment, conscious dialogue with the Mystery that made us, Voegelin's Beginning and Beyond.[1] In Haughton's view, it is nothing tricky or extra, just the consciousness that occurs when one lives from the center of exchange, the nodal point of the relationship with Mystery that defines our inmost human reality.[2] Perhaps the first thing to be said about prayer, therefore, is that it should be natural, spontaneous, easy.

In saying this I am reminded of the many little "women's" books about prayer that domesticate it to chatting with God. Usually I am repulsed by their babyfication, their sunny little kitchens and checkered curtains, but now it strikes me that they do have some wisdom. God does come as a parent, an intimate, a friend. It is far better even to babble to God than to bracket God in sophistication. Still, I don't vote for the model of an intimate tete-a-tete with divinity. I rather choose a variable God, who is the Other at the end of all my self-identifying lines. Mother, Father, Lover, Ground—I cannot begin to list all God's names. Like a Muslim conjuring a mystical 99, I need a rosary to help me count the ways. On good days I can be thankful, joyous, a great singer of praises. On bad days I can grumble, protest, ask for help, still try to praise. Though she slay me, yet will I trust her, I bluster when the weather turns grim. Let her small still voice be my purest music, my heart of hearts requests.

One of the best prayer books I have found is Huub Oosterhuis's *Your Word Is Near*, now almost twenty years old. Its language is hopelessly sexist (and never was the smoothest English translation from Dutch), but it still powerfully conveys a poetic spirit trying wholeheartedly to be honest. Listen, for example, to Oosterhuis's annotations on prayer, and then to his rendering of Job:

> We know nothing about the origin of the phenomenon we call "prayer." Where did we get it from? How did mankind come by it? Prayer is simply there as a matter of course, in all the holy books of all the religions of mankind. It is simply there—it came suddenly, perhaps, or else it just always has been there. Prayer is simply a matter of course in the bible. It was so much taken for granted that, to begin with, Israel had no word for "prayer." The word for praying was rejoicing, laughing, crying, reviling, imploring, according to how one felt. There were hardly any fixed rites, specially privileged places, or strictly prescribed times for prayer in Israel. Everything was allowed—that was the most powerful impulse in this people's relationship with their God. There was no special language for prayer, sacred and sublime. You could pray in every posture and every mode. The God of Israel was quite differ-

ent from all other gods. He was not a god who compelled, made demands and used force. He was not a "mother earth and father heaven" to whom men had to bear sacrifices with their backs bent, not a god who had to be addressed with lowered gaze and muted tongues in a standardized jargon...

Prayer is what Job is doing in the following fragment: Job raised his eyes and called to heaven: I will not keep my mouth shut. I must express the bitterness of my soul—you force me to it. Am I the sea, or a sea monster perhaps, to be locked up and guarded by You? There is no comfort for me, even when I am in bed—you come to scare me with dreams, with visions of terror. I would rather be strangled... What have I done to you, prying watcher of men? Why have you made me your target? And why am I a burden to you? Why can't you forget about my sin? Why don't you overlook my shortcomings?[3]

Job lit out after God, stuck it right to Him. There was no wishy-washy, mealy-mouthed search for proper pieties. What he was, then and there, he let fly. And so should we: Here I am. Take this mess. Let me be. Love me. Help me. I love you—want to, at least. Give me a word. Send forth your spirit. Recreate me. Hush me to quiet. Bring me release.

IN THE SPIRIT

When we pray, we engage the God of the economy of salvation, which is the exchanges with God that bring people healing and divine life. In New Testament terms, this is a work of Jesus' Spirit, the "other paraclete" that he will give the disciples after his departure, as the gospel of John reconstructs it. In the Hebrew Bible, the economy of salvation lies under the guidance of Lady Wisdom, who is very close to the divine Spirit:

During the four centuries that preceded Jesus' coming into our world, a body of Jewish writings now known as the Wisdom literature developed. This literature includes Job and the Proverbs (between 450 and 400 B.C.), numerous Psalms, Quoheleth or Ecclesiastes, Sirach or Ecclesiasticus (c. 187 B.C.) and, in Alexandria, where the Jews were in contact with Hellenistic thought, Wisdom (c. 50 B.C.). The sapiential literature of Hellenized Judaism constitutes a remarkable reflection on Wisdom. In it, Wisdom is brought so close to the Spirit that the realities are almost identified, at least if they are viewed in their action.

This Wisdom comes from God. She is his action for the benefit of his creatures, enabling them to go straight. There is an inclination in God to do good and to desire what is good. Wisdom therefore has a universal extension. In Wis. 1:7 and 8:1, she—or the Spirit—even has a cosmic function, similar to the part that Wisdom played in Stoicism in holding the universe together. The real function of Wisdom, however, is to guide men in accordance with God's will. For this reason, she chose especially to reside in Israel, where she formed God's friends and prophets. She is "the book of the covenant of the Most High God, the law which Moses commanded (us)" (Sir 24:23). The action of Wisdom is therefore very similar to that of the Spirit. They would be identical were it not for the fact that Wisdom does not have what the Spirit has, namely the character of a force or inner energy, the power to transform.[4]

The passage has several interesting implications, especially for women eager to pray well. First, it shows that Jewish monotheism did not lead to a God aloof from creation but a God active in our lives. In the figure of Lady Wisdom, who sometimes seems to be divine and sometimes seems to be a Platonic demiurge or secondary force, later Israelite thought fashioned images of the intelligence by which God wants the world to run. This intelligence was imagined to be feminine, no doubt because it was gracious, lovely, nonviolent. Women serious about praying might reflect on this part of their biblical heritage. Like the ancient Chinese, who thought of the Tao (the Way that runs the world) as more feminine than masculine, the later Israelite thinkers thought of the "reason" that runs through the world as feminine. When things go according to God's plan, they go gently, caringly, with a view to nurturing life rather than forcing it forward.

Second, this feminine quality can remain in specifically Christian reflections on Wisdom and the Spirit if we are willing to read between the lines of the traditional language and speak up for women's rights. For example, Eastern Christianity has spoken of the "energies" of God that enable the Trinity both to remain apart in a strict divinity that creatures can never share and to communicate itself to us creatures in the processes of divinization.[5] The intent of this conception seems similar to the intent of the Hebrew notion of Lady Wisdom: to bring the divine into the realm of human experience, human interiority. The Eastern Fathers who worked out the notion of the uncreated energies put little stress on feminine language, but if we focus on the effect of communicating the energies we find ourselves bringing forward such figures as the brooding of divine life, the nurture of divine love, the education of human hearts—all quite maternal activities. Insofar as prayer is opening oneself to God's life, saying yes to God's offer of divinization, it is like a child rushing into her mother's arms, an older daughter responding to her mother's friendship.

Third, the Western Christian notions of the Spirit can also pass through a feminist transformer, as Congar, the author quoted above, anticipates in speaking of the *power* attributed to the Spirit in the Hebrew Bible. The power of the Christian Spirit (most dramatically portrayed in Acts' description of Pentecost) is only unfeminine if one keeps to old stereotypes of femininity. (Similarly, the Wisdom of either Testament is only unmasculine if one keeps to old stereotypes of masculinity.) In other cultures (Hindu India, for example), the forceful side of divinity (*shakti*) is depicted as feminine. So we can conceive Christ's Spirit as a mothering force that is ardent like fire, strong like a mighty wind. We need not shift to a masculine pronoun when we speak of the powerful spirit who creates, cleanses, and helps Christ's Body. In fact, a good half-way house on the road to a completely liberated language for God would have "She" as the preferred pronoun for the Spirit.

Applying this to prayer, I would place a feminist accent on the recent pentecostal or charismatic renewal of many Christian bodies, seeing their return to forceful prayer as a reinvigoration of Lady Wisdom. When the Spirit seizes the inmost heart, She wills a transformation that would fill the personality with gifts (charismata) of both prayer and action. In the Spirit, then, women can pray: Come Lord Jesus. Make this broken world whole.

MEDITATION

A good form of prayer for beginners who are still groping after the leadings of the Spirit is meditation: thinking over the truths of faith, and then placing the fruits of one's ruminations before God. To grow strong in Christian faith we must have made the core Christian truths our own. We cannot live adult religious lives with the schooling of children. But the sort of study that best nourishes Christian maturation is not the dry, head-only reflection that the academies teach. It is the rumination, tasting, pondering that traditionally went by the name "lectio divina," divine reading, in which the heart is as prominent as the intellect. Indeed, it is what Pascal called "the reasons of the heart," the logic of love, that we are trying to discern. So the Bible, God's Word, has traditionally been the main material of divine reading, and surely it should continue to be central today, even though we must beware of its patriarchalism. As long as we make sure that no biblical passage leads us to depreciate women or deny that women are as much the images of God as men, we can meditate on the Bible with singular profit.

After the Bible, the Christian spiritual classics offer fine meditational fare. Despite the cultural distance at which many of them stand from us, the spiritual classics can be good grist for our mill, our nurture in the Spirit. Consider, for example, the following passage from *The Interior Castle* of St. Teresa of Avila. The saint, whom the Roman Catholic church has made a "doctor" or especially authoritative teacher, is discussing how God communicates to us: "I do not mean . . . that he speaks to us and calls us in the precise way which I shall describe later; his appeals come through the conversations of good people, or from sermons, or through the reading of good books; and there are many other ways, of which you have heard, in which God calls us. Or they come through sicknesses and trials, or by means of truths which God teaches us at times when we are engaged in prayer; however feeble such prayers may be, God values them highly. You must not despise this first favour, sisters, nor be disconsolate, even though you have not responded immediately to the Lord's call; for his Majesty is quite prepared to wait for many days, and even years, especially when he sees we are persevering and have good desires."[6]

Teresa, a woman of extraordinary spiritual discernment, a mystic of the first order, manages here, as in so many other passages in her writings, to speak clearly and encouragingly to even the humblest beginner. For her God comes in myriad ways, speaks through dozens of messengers and situations. Moreover, God is patient, contenting herself with our good desires, enduring our stumbling starts, our slow ignition. When I read passages such as this and let them sink down to the center of myself, I feel less discouraged about the poor quality of my religious life. Teresa is suggesting that God may be more eloquent and patient than I had thought.

In our relations with our kids, our troubles at work, our fears about the future, God may be scattering hints, helps, breadcrumbs. Teresa herself was a slow starter and for many years quite worldly. What she had going for her, in addition to God's special love, was a strong, vibrant, very practical personality. She reminds me of nothing so much as one of those mighty biblical women, a Judith or Esther, whose "strong right arm" slew the enemy and strengthened the people. Not for Teresa any self-image of fluttering or sniveling. Her God was an almost rapacious lover, a force riveting her to the point of ecstasy. But this mystical life had humble, ordinary beginnings: persevering and having good desires. Tasting Teresa's encouraging teachings and chewing them through, today's religious feminist might find much consolation.

The same with another strong woman, Simone Weil, whose meditations have won exceptional praise for their honesty and depth. In the passage I quote she is speaking about the way to follow the Spirit's leadings, so that we read and study as our inner needs dictate: "I had never read any mystical works, because I had never felt any call to read them. In reading as in other things I have always striven to practice obedience. There is nothing more favorable to intellectual progress, for as far as possible I only read what I am hungry for at the moment when I have an appetite for it, and then I do not read, I *eat*. God in his mercy had prevented me from reading the mystics, so that it should be evident to me that I had not invented this absolutely unexpected contact.

"Yet I still half refused, not my love but my intelligence. For it seemed to me certain, and I still think so today, that one can never wrestle enough with God if one does so out of pure regard for the truth. Christ likes us to prefer truth to him because, before being Christ, he is truth. If one turns aside from him to go toward the truth, one will not go far before falling into his arms."[7]

For Simone Weil, we should meditate (read reflectively, personally) as our inner hungers dictate. This entails a sort of obedience to the Spirit working within us. And when we practice such obedience we find that we are not so much reading as devouring food our soul craves. (Here I am reminded of the image of Revelation 10:9: take the scroll and eat it.) Weil's Jewish heritage comes through in her figure of wrestling with God to discern the truth. But her special gift in this passage, I think, is the notion that we cannot but fall into Christ's arms, if we are pursuing the truth. So, for example, if we are honestly pursuing the truth of sexual relationships, how men and women really ought to stand to one another, we cannot but move deeper into the Wisdom of God, the Word of God, even though temporarily we may find ourselves on the outs with Church leaders. "Think on these things, sisters," Simone Weil might say. "Taste and see the joy and peace, the freedom and care, they offer at the fine point of your soul."

CONTEMPLATION

The stage of prayer that often follows on meditation is contemplation. Frequently people who have ruminated on passages of Scripture and the classics for a few years find that this stream is running dry. They have had enough words, thoughts, reasonings. The hunger in their hearts has become stronger than the hunger in their minds, and the hunger in their hearts is to regard God whole, abide with God simply, and just love God heart to heart. They may want to do this while using such physical foci as icons or pastoral scenes, or they may want no images at all and prefer the divine darkness. Either way, as Simone Weil suggested, they should be obedient to their inner hunger. There is no commandment from God that we meditate on and on. The command from God is that we love. Alternatively, when Paul enjoined constant prayer, he did not imply that it had to be meditation. Indeed, he did not specify any particular form. So the famous anonymous Russian pilgrim, who set out to find an answer to Paul's enjoinment, found himself being instructed by spiritual fathers in the Jesus prayer or some variant: the constant repetition of "Lord Jesus Christ, Son of the Living God, have mercy on me a sinner."[8] So a pilgrim today might receive similar advice from an Orthodox spiritual mother.[9] In both cases the goal of the spiritual advice would not be a wooden recitation of the formula but a recitation that so holds the senses that the formula gradually penetrates the heart and becomes an inner chant in rhythm with the heart's beating.

The imageless modes of contemplation have played a major role in Christian teaching about prayer, East and West, especially when one begins to talk about the ways that God purifies the serious seeker, that She may become as real as sensible things. The roots of this imageless or negative contemplation lie in the negative or apophatic theological tradition, which is powered by the conviction that God is always more unlike than like what we say, imagine, or think about God. What we say, think, or imagine is not necessarily wrong, but it always falls far short of the infinite Mystery of divinity. That the Word of God would take flesh and dwell among us proves that the divinity, far from despising material forms, is willing to use anything that will carry its love. But if we are to deal with God intimately, we must learn how God is in herself. In herself God is not material, finite, incarnate. In herself God is "beyond": more than the best that our most profound analogies can convey.[10]

If this is so, then many people who are serious about prayer and want to love God deeply and realistically will find themselves drawn to a regard of God, to a stance toward God, that tries to undercut the busy-ness of the mouth, the imagination, the mind. They will feel drawn to the simplest of waitings upon God, the starkest attendings. "God" will be something blank, dark, opaque. The mind will have no handle on this God, so the mind will protest. "Don't bother much about the mind," the masters of negative prayer counsel. "Just keep the heart loving." For the heart, following the initiatives of the Spirit, is going far beyond the mind, far deeper. The heart, the center of the whole personality, is opening to the spiritual presence of God, the divine love-life. This divine love-life is the most precious force in the universe, according to such apophatic masters as the anonymous author of the medieval classic, *The Cloud of Unknowing*. Attending, waiting upon the dark divine love-life, is the best thing one can do, for the world as well as oneself.

It is this conviction that lies behind the traditional Catholic support of the contemplative life, monasticism. The monks and nuns who give themselves over to constant prayer are making a way for God in the wilderness, making straight a divine path. When they are truly dedicated to deep prayer, they become real-symbols, living sacraments, of the presence of the divine otherness. Paradoxically enough, the saint, however removed physically, is close to the heart of the most important historical action. The only trouble with the traditional Christian defense of this truth is its tendency to suggest that deep prayer can only occur in removed monasteries. Were the ideal to be set before all the people of God (as a fully catholic ideal always is), it would be completely unexceptionable.

For, all of us, however stumbling and dirty, have a spark of desire for what is ultimately real, genuinely holy. Contemplative prayer is merely the fanning of this spark so that it becomes (to use John of the Cross's imagery) a living flame of love. Before the spark can become a living flame it must pass through very trying dark nights, in which first the senses and then the very ground of the spirit are purified. Yet as long as we have any spiritual life at all, the slightest bit of faith-hope-love, we hunger for this purification, sensing that it would make us what we most deeply want to be. True enough, most of us are not willing to pay the price of deep purification, so our "want" remains something of a velleity. But I have found a solid want, more than a velleity, in a great many women, the majority of them neither learned nor advantaged. Often it is their troubles that have pushed them down toward the depths. Often it is by crying out from their depths that they have experienced the real God—the one beyond all pleasantries and saccharines, the devouring lover of Teresa and Simone. Contemplation—loving intercourse—with this God is no idle pastime. It is a re-creation at the very roots of one's being.

ICONOGRAPHY

Because they had taken the doctrine of the Incarnation to heart, many Christian masters of prayer defended the use of icons— images of Christ, Mary, and the saints. If God had taken flesh, then material representations of God could be holy ways to commune with divine Goodness. Icons were not in themselves to be worshiped. The traditional masters were not at all confused about that. But an icon could participate in the holy aura of the reality it represented, and it could be a wonderful way of drawing the person who wanted to worship God into contemplating the divine beauty and mystery, the plan of salvation.

All this still remains quite true today. People wanting to pray deeply, to immerse themselves in the Christian mysteries, can very profitably betake themselves to a holy image. Placing themselves before the solemn visage, bowing or making some other act of reverence, they can ride their senses toward the simple love of God that is "behind" the image, and responsible for the beauty and good works of the person being venerated. An icon venerator is not the same as a person in an art gallery. The motivation behind her gazing is not aesthetic—although there is nothing wrong with admiring the great beauty of many of the icons—but religious, a desire to hallow the ultimate sanctity of God's Mystery. Because God's mystery is the objective, the venerator is not an idolator, any more than most "pagan" venerators of trees, stones, animals, or ancestors have been idolators.

Let me try to make this concrete, and thereby show how a mature person like one of my students might use the iconographic tradition today. Recently I purchased a beautiful book on icons. I wanted the interpretive studies that several contributors had written about the different schools of Byzantine iconography, but I wanted the stunning reproductions of famous images even more. Thumbing through the book now, I come across "Virgin of Vladimir," which even I (a very rank amateur in art) have seen numerous times—it is, for instance, reminiscent of "Our Lady of Perpetual Help." It is a good-sized picture (104 x 69 cm), tempera, and thought to have been painted in Constantinople about 1131. Like many icons, its artist is unknown (anonymity often was the rule). Presently it is in the Tretyakov Gallery in Moscow. To say the least, it is a striking icon, so I propose first to describe it and then to essay a "contemplation" (holistic religious appreciation put into words) that might represent something of what a devout contemporary Christian feminist could make of it.[11]

The picture is of the Virgin with Christ child. Its main colors are black and gold. The virgin wears a black cloak, apparently long and flowing, that comes over her head in close-fitting fashion like a mantle, so that it comes to within a half-inch of her dark eyebrows. A border of gold around the edge of the mantle gives it a regal look. The Christ child nuzzles against the Virgin, cheek to cheek. His little robe is of gold, with black touches. He is bare-headed with curly hair, and he has large dark eyes and full red lips. He reaches one dark little arm to his mother's clavicle for support while the other goes round her neck.

The focus of the icon, however, is the Virgin's countenance— more precisely, her eyes. They are dark, almond shaped, and mysterious. She has a long, slightly aquiline nose, a small red mouth, and a generally oval face. Her expression is what makes the icon exquisite. Like the expression of the Mona Lisa, it is puzzling, intriguing, mysterious. But where the Mona Lisa seems on the verge of a knowing smile or a hint of flirtation, the Virgin seems on the verge of sorrow. Her eyes have glimpsed something of the future that lies in store for her baby, and for herself. At least one of her seven swords of suffering has already pierced her.

Still, the icon is more peaceful than dolorous. The Virgin's sadness is banked by a deep acceptance. Perhaps the arms of the child comfort her. Certainly his cheek against her own bespeaks their utter intimacy. For the East, the Virgin above all has been the Theotokos, the God-bearer. It is because he took flesh from the Virgin that the Word became our Savior. The tie between divinity and this woman, the acme of our species, is as close as the rub of the child's cheek, and as soft, intimate, and unpretentious. The Virgin's eyes penetrate the onlooker's soul. "Do you know what part you will play, have played, in the drama we are to suffer?"

Today's feminist, conscious of the ambiguous use the Church has made of Mary in its teachings about women, probably does best to let her thoughts fade. Before the icon, I let my heart take over, turning the beauty and sadness toward sisterhood. Anyone who has held a baby can capture the first level of the Virgin's sensations. The warmth and give of the little weight she holds is life immediate, life still close to the wonder of birth. Women know life immediately. If we wish, we can center down to the place where life begins. This life is bound to suffer—perhaps that is its only surety. But somehow its suffering only makes it more precious. It should not suffer most of what it will, so we cannot gaze on it except sadly. But an almost fierce power in us wills that it endure and triumph over the evils that will afflict it. That a baby such as Jesus could one day take to himself life's worst evils and crush them with pure love is staggering. Anyone at all serious will ponder the Virgin of Vladimir with deep reverence and gratitude.

THERAPY

I have been speaking of prayer as something that ought to flow in us naturally, something that goes forward under the guidance of a Spirit quite like Lady Wisdom, something that has meditative and contemplative phases, and something that Eastern iconography understood very well. Implicit in all of this discussion, I hope, has been the helical model of self-transcendence. We are free to pursue prayer as perhaps the most holistic of our forms of communing with the divine Mystery (and so engaging our goal). All the drive and thrust in us for growth, for knowing what is real and embracing what is good, can surge forward in ardent contemplation. On the other hand, we shall quickly find that honest prayer is careful —aware that it is mainly an exercise in exchange, mindful that the Other has the right to make demands, sensitive to the priority of the Creator in everything that is ultimate. As well, mature prayer is social, an act that cannot evade the world and does not want to. So, for example, a careful contemplation of the Virgin of Vladimir soon brings to mind the sufferings that have stamped Christian history: the sufferings of Mary's child, of Mary herself, and of all the members, actual or potential, of Christ's Body. Millions of these members suffer today in our own period of history. Millions more await the full takeover of the Resurrection, the time when God will be all in all. In so solitary a moment as contemplation before a lovely icon, the Christian worshiper rediscovers her thousand connections to the rest of creation. The Mystery she contemplates is exactly what we are all in together.

The highest *telos* or perfecting end of prayer is the praise and adoration of God. This is what tradition says the Seraphim and Cherubim sing unceasingly. The Eastern tradition that undergirds the most splendid iconography makes a great deal of the Trisagion, the triple-holy of Isaiah's vision that has become a high point in the Divine Liturgy. Isaiah is describing the God of the covenant: "I saw the Lord sitting upon a throne, high and lifted up; and his train filled the temple. Above him stood the seraphim; each had six wings: with two he covered his face, and with two he covered his feet, and with two he flew. And one called out to the other and said: 'Holy, holy, holy is the Lord of hosts; the whole earth is full of his glory'" (Isaiah 6:1–3). Women praying out of Jewish or Christian faith today have every right to appropriate this heritage. Their prayer, too, can aspire to the pinnacles of praise where God's power and purity receive their full due. Today the diction of such praise may be very different from Isaiah's. The gender of the God-image and angel-form may vary. But the core of the lifting of mind and heart can be identical: Praise her, for her wondrous gifts, for her wonderful self.

People who pray are not always on the heights, however, and do not have to be to pray well. If a prayer without moments of pure adoration would be suspect, so would a prayer without moments in which the needs of the worshiper are to the fore. So it is right and just, proper and helpful to salvation to speak of prayer's therapies. We go to prayer frequently enough because we need healing. Did we not receive such healing more than now and then, most of us would not persevere. And what form is such healing likely to take? I can only use my own experience to interpret the mainstream of the tradition, and in my experience the healing of prayer usually comes as a reorientation, detachment, and centering down. Many of my ills are due to bad perspective, a loss of proportion. Prayer regularly turns me around, reminds me where the sun is, the source of my hopes. Many other of my ills come from desire, impure ambition. Prayer regularly reminds me that one thing alone is necessary, my best effort to love. I suffer because I have gotten myself, or been pushed by others, out of joint. I have become dispersed, scattered, fragmented. Prayer centers me down, recollects my fragments, puts me back together. The hallmarks of a prayer session I call good are the peace and joy it leaves. These are more sober than dancing, more realistic than fanciful, more blank than specified. "Somehow," they say, "all will be well. You have grace enough to keep going."

It is part of our Christian birthright, then, to bring our battered selves before the Spirit-healer. She is used to washing what is sordid, watering what is dry, pouring balm on sore wounds. The sins that make us sordid can be cleansed in her deep quiet, whether sins of arrogant over-freedom or sins of fearful under-care. The depression, loss of hope, the sense that life is passing us by—all that makes us like a desert floor, parched and split—can wash away and green shoots spring up. The worries we have for a spouse, a child, a friend, an unlovely self can stop chafing. And this is not just my testimony, something I'm trying to pretty into balanced little sentences. It is the testimony of the whole cloud of witnesses who have gone out into the desert to pray, confronted the demanding eyes of the icons, listened to the Word with hearts open to conceive. Thus Dietrich Bonhoeffer, who gave his life to oppose the Nazis, once wrote of pain: "Stifter once said 'pain is a holy angel, who shows treasures to men which otherwise remain forever hidden; through him men have become greater than through all joys of the world.' It must be so and I tell this to myself in my present position over and over again—the pain of longing, which often can be felt even physically, must be there, and we shall not and need not talk it away. But it needs to be overcome every time, and thus is an even holier angel than the one of pain, that is the one of joy in God."[12]

PRACTICE

The proof of prayer, like many other important things, is in action. All the theory in the world won't be of much use unless we set to work and find the theory verified. In the case of prayer, where many people say that the only teacher is the Holy Spirit, practice becomes doubly important. Indeed, about the only thing one can say, without fear of contradiction, is that prayer must become regular, constant, a staple of one's life, if it is to bear the fruit it should. Let us therefore try to deal with the problem of practice: getting prayer into one's routine, making it regular and habitual, working out an honest personal voice. This would not have been an easy task in any time, but today it is compounded by the busyness of most Americans' lives, the strong competition for our time. For after work and sleep, family life, meals, exercise, recreation, and many other possibilities contend for the few hours left. Most of these choices are good enough in themselves, meriting an excellent brief, an elaborate argument. The argument for prayer, by contrast, is very plain: If you do not do this, you will not become fully human, conscious of the height and breadth and depth of God's love.

I like to capitalize on the rhythms of my day. These dictate that early morning and late evening will be quiet times, when I seem to pray best. So I try to make early morning and late evening contemplative, reflective, and meditative. Early morning has the advantage of getting the day off to a good start. I'm not a quick waker, so often my early morning prayer is rather dull, a simple praise and petition of God, without many refinements. We have a little solar house powered by a sunspace, the roof of which is glass. I love to watch the day dawn. Sometimes the moon or the morning star is still lingering. Often the dawn comes with lovely streaks of grey, pink, blue, or gold. Kansas has a big sky, with fine sunrises and sunsets. I try to use these to praise God and bless the day. Out my window several large trees report on the season. In summer they are lush. In winter they are gnarled. The tiny fresh leaves of spring seem exceedingly fragile. The wild colors of fall are a painter's fancy. It is a beautiful world in the early morning, and I try to use this beauty to reanimate my faith in the goodness of creation, the possibility of salvation.

Late in the evening, which is my more naturally contemplative time, people dominate the mental horizon. Most days I have contended with a great many people, and often this leaves me feeling the worse for wear. Teaching is the joyous center of my day. Almost always it gives me energy. The other, more administrative contacts tend to be draining, largely because so much human folly intrudes. There are the talkers who will do anything rather than make a decision and get something done. There are the backbiters, who think that pulling other people apart somehow will consolidate themselves. There are the faithless, who exude a corrosive skepticism. There are the little people, students and staff, who too often fall into the cracks. And, of course, there are the generous, humorous, good-hearted colleagues who make the university worth while. At night most of them pass by my window in review. Their needs, causes, sins are the main fuel of my reflections. As I consider how I have interacted with them, the "mystery of salvation" becomes quite pregnant. Usually my tally is rather inconclusive. To find grace abounding over sin takes a solid infusion of faith. By the time I am ready to let the whole notion of tallying go, pass it over to some more far-seeing analyst, it is again clear that I shall only be justified by faith and have little merit I can call my own.

Some people find this sort of reflection irksome, and I sympathize with that. However, to come at the end of my ruminations to the opaque mystery of God, find once again that everything is grace, is not a sad or defeatist conclusion. On the contrary, it is a return to simple realism. What wearies me is trying to carry the whole world, trying to play God. What refreshes me is letting go, seeing the smallness of my mission. Like the alcoholic, I need the wisdom to distinguish between the things I can change and the things out of my hands. The things I can change tend to locate in myself. The things out of my hands tend to locate in other people's freedom. I have yet fully to accept the fact that some people will insist on using their freedom to their own hurt. Indeed, some will insist on trying to use it to my hurt. I can't convert people who don't want to live in the light, who love the light less than they fear it. I can't get very far with people who don't want to canonize love and prefer a reign of law, or ever a raw fight for advantage. I can only try to do good, promote friendship, advance what I take to be the truth. This, and some realistic self-protection, are what I presently take to be the part of wisdom.

So I find myself concluding, again, with admiration for teachings such as those of Ignatius Loyola that tell me to work as if everything depended on God. I am a typically middle-class American, driven and overextended. For me the lilies of the field are a sermon almost always to the point. On the other hand, there is the rest of Loyola's teaching: Pray as if everything depended on yourself. That I find, is a straight path to justification by faith, the priority of grace, and quiet adoration in the cloud of unknowing. Putting it into practice means seeing how little health there is in me, realizing that sending God my desire to love is probably the best prayer I will ever make.

CARTE BLANCHE

Because serious prayer sets us before God immediately, with no buffers, it can be discouraging. Sensing even the slightest bit of

God's holiness, we grow acutely aware of our own untidiness, our deep roots of sin. The dark nights that purify the courageous person remove any notion of self-sufficiency. Far below the level most assertiveness training targets, we learn that God has all the priority in the religious life. This is not a disheartening lesson when we have finally appropriated it. In the long run it is a great cause for celebration. But in the short run, when we are not sure about our responsibilities and still think that bootstrap operations have merit, naked openness to the Spirit can be sorely trying. If half the people who quit serious prayer do so because they fail to negotiate the transition from meditation to contemplation, the other half quit because they get discouraged at their lack of "progress," their inability to clear the moral slate. Applying the standards of worldly success, they expect a quick and handsome return on their investment. When this comes in ways they initially find unattractive, they often betake themselves to kinder gurus or treat themselves to a shopping spree.

I think it important, therefore, to face early on the carte blanche that faith and prayer demand. This carte blanche is not the magic card that allows you to charge all the self-indulgence you can muster. It is the unconditional trust in God that God's unconditional love of us solicits, as the condition for a sanctifying exchange. In the spirit of Job one comes to say, "Though He slay me yet will I trust Him." In the spirit of Paul one proclaims: "We know that in everything God works for good with those who love him, who are called according to his purpose. . . For I am sure that neither death, nor life, nor angels, nor principalities, nor things present, nor things to come, nor powers, nor height, nor depth, nor anything else in all creation, will be able to separate us from the love of God in Christ Jesus our Lord" (Romans 8:28, 38–39).

The quotation is extreme, as was Paul's faith. For him the Christ event had shown God's love to be unconditional: "He who did not spare his own Son but gave him up for us all, will he not also give us all things with him?" (Romans 8:32). The best analogy in human terms is probably motherly love. Even when her child is a criminal, a good mother finds it hard to stop loving that child. She doesn't excuse what was done, but she is more than willing to forgive the harm caused her. It is a peculiar attitude, beyond the reach of lawyers and rationalists. Because the mother knows the child so well, from the first days when they shared a single life, the mother can forgive far more than those who only know the child objectively. Because she has done more for the child than other people, she is ready to overlook the child's stupidities.

Jesus captured much of this peculiarity in his parable of the prodigal son (Luke 15). The parable really is about the father more than the son. The father is so good that the son can never alienate him, no matter how outrageous the son's behavior. Jesus is saying that God is like that. Nothing can separate us from the love of God—not because of us, but because of God. God simply is so good that she will never stop loving us. The slightest sign that we have "come to ourselves," as the son does when he contemplates the pigs living better than he, is enough to make God rush out to meet us, gather rings for our fingers, kill the fatted calf and make merry.

I think that these glimpses of God's transcendent love are what keep me committed to Christianity. I simply don't find them in any other place. Compared to their depth and dazzle, the insights of most secular thinkers are baby food. At times I need baby food, so I don't mean to despise any help that I or anyone else can get. But in my best times I need a word that slashes to joint and marrow, comes to grips with the deepest issues of ignorance, finitude, mortality, and evil. Philosophies that don't plumb these depths of the human condition are sophomoric, the initially impressive but soon unsatisfying productions of wise fools. The peasant who broods over the turn of the seasons, the time to rejoice and the time to weep, is far wiser than the sophisticate (businessman or academic, churchman or feminist) who has no concern for ultimate meaning, and feels nothing stir when Paul hymns God's love.

Moreover, the carte blanche of faith which takes God's unconditional love to heart, setting it like a mezzuzah above the lintel, is nothing merely speculative or ideal. On the contrary, it is the most practical sort of orientation. Consider the mother contemplating an unwed pregnant daughter. If she is superficial, the mother mainly worries about what the neighbors will think. If she is mature, her heart goes out to the daughter and the new life. If she is profound, she broods in her depths about wrongdoing, asking the Mystery to show her its sense, stir her conviction that no misstep need be fatal. Consider the man come to a new job who finds signs it will prove a disaster. He has moved his family 3000 miles only to join a flock of turkeys. If he is superficial, he worries about his image of shrewdness. If he is mature, he feels heartsick at the useless sacrifices his wife and children have made. If he is profound, he searches the tides of ultimacy, seeking a current that could give them all a reason to hope. Finding it, he laughs at his foolishness and breaks out like Tertullian and Kierkegaard: I believe because it is absurd.

6 *WORK*

With the topic of work we begin to focus on the two central panels of our practical tableau. Work and love were Freud's nominees for the crucial activities or capacities that determine our mental health. In his mind, the person who could work creatively and carry off sexual love was in relatively good shape. I think that Freud's slate was too skimpy, but if he could now admit that prayer and politics also bear intrinsically on mental health, I would gladly accede to the importance of work and love.

Since work is an area feminist spirituality conceived as self-transcendence must illumine if it is to pay its way, let us begin our probings of work by dealing with art. Perhaps it is the ultimate character of our last reflection on the carte blanche at the foundations of prayer that prompts me to begin here. For certainly art is one of the highest aspirations of work—one of the things whose difficulty of realization throws the observer of the workscene into depression, and calls for bedrock faith. If one looks out upon the world of work, in the United States or abroad, art is not what first strikes the eye. In the next section we will deal with the suffering that first strikes the eye. Here let us try to make our spiritual model mesh with one of the loftiest ideals of the worker: being involved in the making of something beautiful.

Something beautiful can also be useful, so I do not mean to begin by setting art against utility. On the other hand, I want to concentrate on beauty, not utility. Something is beautiful when it combines grace and power, pleases the sense and satisfies the mind.

"Beauty" is so basic a notion, however, that I find myself struggling to find anything more primitive. Let me therefore forego side-trips into aesthetics and content myself with a commensensical notion of beauty, something on which cab drivers and painters might agree. My thesis is that unless our work has a solid relation to such beauty we are much less fulfilled than we know in our bones we ought to be. Work is not simply for money, mass-production, the supplying of goods. Work by nature is something that connects with the worker's center, our heart-mind-soul-and-strength.

I therefore see art as a most important aspect of work, something whose lack immediately makes a work dolorous. If a person is in a situation that forces her to produce products that are ugly and frustrates all her aspirations toward elegance and pleasure, she is tasting something hellish, the denial of what she has been made for. Fortunately, many rather ordinary works can be carried out in an artistic manner if the worker has the wit and encouragement to attempt it. For example, teaching certainly can become artistic if the teacher is willing to develop the communication skills and vision that would render her expositions both pleasing and significant. Many teachers in fact work very hard for such effects, and quite a few become impressive artists. Almost always they love their work, and their love grows apace with their art. By the time they are masters, even in modest degree, their work is something they do for its intrinsic value. Of course they want to be paid, need to be paid, but they will teach for far less pay than they might receive in a non-teaching situation. For they know that in a non-teaching situation they would be different people, less than their full selves.

The art of teaching, however, is fairly well known. To speak of intrinsic value and the identification of the worker with the work in the classroom will raise few eyebrows. Harder cases are things like waiting on tables, secretarial work, construction work, and parenting. Because these seem to be ordinary, unprestigious kinds of work, we are slower to think of their artistic possibilities. Yet, as soon as we put our mind to it, we see that one can wait on table graciously or one can bang the silver. One can keep elegant files and type perfect letters, or one can leave everything a little off-center. There are construction workers who economize their outlay of force and build with tidiness. There are parents with a knack for disciplining their kids, delighting their kids, loving their kids to full health.

In each of these positive cases, an artist is at work. Just as the difference between mere food and haute cuisine is hard to miss, so is the difference between the artistic waitress, secretary, construction worker, or parent and her less gifted counterpart. With mature art comes ease, competence, fluency. The artist makes her work a medium of herself, a way of being and growing. Thus to have work that is not at least somewhat artistic is to face the dismal prospect that one's major doing may be a great obstacle to one's growing. Until we can make the time we put in at the office and the time we lavish on the kids something plausibly conducive to our own development, we lie within a thrice of depression.

All praise to those, therefore, who labor for the liberation of work, especially the work of society's most burdened. Often women are a majority of this class, as women are a majority in three of the four unprestigious work categories mentioned above. Sometimes a very small shift can make a great difference in the artistic possibilities of a job. Things like flex-time, inviting a worker's initiative, granting increased responsibility, and praising artistic achievements can even make a bad situation bearable. For then the worker at least feels she is contributing something to the art of the whole enterprise and so is not wholly deadened.

SUFFERING

Workers ought to be free to do their work at least somewhat artistically. When they are not—when the work-situation is so stacked against art that the worker might as well be a machine—they have a solid grievance against the economic structure. Similarly, workers ought to be able to love their work and make it a means of exchange with other people, a means of building up the network of relations that helps all parties in a venture flourish. When they are not able to love their own work and find it putting them at odds with other people, destroying exchange and relationship, they have another solid grievance against the economic structure. In both the capitalist and the communist economic systems, such grievances are all too common. Because the capitalistic system subordinates the worker to the firm's making a profit, it is ever liable to stomp on art and social service. Because the communist system subordinates the worker to crude, ideological notions of the common good, it regularly crushes creativity and incentive. The capitalistic system is extremely vulnerable to prostitution: making junk that will sell rather than products that are beautiful and fulfill society's basic needs. The communist system is extremely vulnerable to inefficiency, red tape, and the worship of false social needs (e.g., massive military weapons).

The world over, more workers suffer distorting, alienating work conditions than enjoy jobs where their spirits can soar. Rare indeed is the economic system, large or small, that balances individual initiative with an effective concern for the common good, beauty and utility. It is instructive to contemplate the economic systems of small-scale, nonliterate societies, because they have regularly managed to develop workers of great skill who make basic implements or produce basic goods that are remarkably beautiful. On the other hand, it would be sheer romanticism to overlook the severe limitations of most such societies in terms of education, health care, and the like. What we seem to need, therefore, is enough flexibility to maintain the world wide communications we have developed in the contemporary world without losing opportunities for individuals to work artistically. That would be a minimal goal. A maximal goal would be to design an economic system in which the majority of the people had work that was fulfilling.

For herself, the contemporary American woman has the hard task of finding how work lends itself to self-transcendence. She certainly is free to seek work that is fulfilling, in which she can make something beautiful or contribute to the improvement of a human whole. She certainly is right to want work that she can love, feel proud of, and come to each day with zest. On the other hand, the hard facts are that most systems do not welcome her the way they welcome a comparable man and are seriously warped by sexism. The 62 cents a woman earns compared to each male dollar is the epitome that says it all. So a working woman realistically must prepare her soul for suffering, either in her own personal experience or in the experience of those whose fates she cannot overlook. That is why politics is inevitable. Those with eyes that see have to notice that something is systemically wrong, and those with consciences that work have to move to change that something.

The women who pass through my classes usually work at least part-time. For most of them a single salary is not enough to pay their family's way. Single parents are even more starkly up against it. For them the 62-cent dollar is especially cruel and worry is a daily companion. So I find the spiritualities that overlook women's present suffering—the long haul that lies between where we are now and where we hope to end up—seriously deficient. This sometimes puts me on the outs with irreligious feminists, as it once did when Betty Friedan disagreed with me publicly.

The occasion was a day given over to women's issues. I had traveled from Wichita to Topeka to be a principal speaker. Betty Friedan was the main draw who gave the plenary address the first night and was the glamor participant in the day's panels. She took exception to my saying that I found religion a valuable resource for women whose present circumstances were especially trying. I had tried to make it clear that I knew the dangers of religion, the slippery slopes to "the opiate of the people" and "pie in the sky." "What, though," I said, "are women to do in this mid-time, when their daily reality at work and at home may be terribly bleak? Can we not try to provide them some of the traditional consolations of the major religious traditions, which have addressed bigger perspectives and deeper resources that somewhat mitigate evil's sting?" Friedan did not come to grips with the intellectual content of this question and suggestion. She merely pushed it aside with rhetoric, asserting that she wanted no part in defeatist sentiments, no focus not thoroughly this-worldly. However, she also professed certitude that women's issues would prevent the election of Ronald Reagan, so I didn't feel I had been rebuked by a major prophet.

Still, the memory rankles, and I feel little different today than I did on the day of the debate. I think a philosophy that cannot contend with the suffering people have right now, suffering that no set of programs however laudable is going to be in place in time to remove, is completely unrealistic and inadequate. Any philosophy worth its salt, in my view, is soteriological: it struggles to bring forth a love and care that can support the weak, help the suffering, honor all people right now by bringing them a word and example of Lady Wisdom, God's Spirit of peace and joy.

UNDERLYINGS

The soteriological power of an adequate economic system would most directly show in its help to people who work in society's least attractive jobs. Such help might come in the form of direct raises, improvements in salary and working conditions. It might also come in the form of the bigger perspectives and deeper resources I mentioned. The structural forms of such a better system have been hinted, or elaborated fully, in numerous works. Economists would be much better placed to discourse on this theme than I. In my small range of reading such names as E.F. Schumacher, Herman E. Daly, Barbara Ward, and Robert Heilbroner stand out. The first three have proposed economic reforms that would better take into account the ecological realities of present day life, and the global interconnectedness of today's economic systems, than do the dominant theories of the Northern nations. As well, all three make a solid place for religious, aesthetic, and personalist values.[1] Heilbroner seems a good guide to the via media between Marxism and centrist capitalism that we probably need for any thorough humanization of work.[2]

The bigger perspectives and deeper resources of religion are not an alternative to better work-systems. Were they taken to heart by those with economic power, religious insights could become strong goals to a wholesale economic reform. But even when they are not taken to heart by the movers and shakers, they can ameliorate the condition of the underlyings, give those presently being ground down ways to renew their senses of self-worth and hope. At times this access to values that undercut the worker's oppressive working conditions can be as simple as the memory of "home," the physical or spiritual place the worker longs to be. This was so for Hannah Morgan, a mountain woman from Harlan County, Kentucky, who had left to find work in cities like Chicago and Dayton.

The cities tended to erode her joy, but in her dreams at night and by day she would go back to her mountain home, retie herself to her roots:

> She desperately needed the money she earned. Her husband had found a job as a packer in a warehouse, and between the two of them they barely managed to get by—and send some dollars to

their respective families: "We didn't come to Chicago to walk on
sidewalks and run out of the way of crazy drivers and inhale smoke
and ride on buses so crowded that you stand for an hour—before
you get to the factory, where you stand all day long. We came to
Chicago because we wanted to make some money, and come back
with it to our home, and live in Harlan County, and work on the
land. We thought that if we could just save a few hundred dollars,
then we wouldn't be so close to the poorhouse; that means having
zero dollars, and it's winter; and you've run out of the food you've
put up, and you're hungry; and the chickens have stopped laying,
and you can't build up more of a debt at the store; and your family
is not in good shape either; and so all you can do is hold your stomach and wait until the hunger pains go away, and then you're tired,
and you feel weak, but you don't desire food—it's strange.

"Every day in that factory I would think to myself, I would talk
to myself. I would remind myself—freedom, later on. So would
my husband, when he was breaking his back in that cold, dark
warehouse; he would tell himself that it would be worth all the
pain, in the end. Half the day I wasn't in Chicago; I was in my
thoughts. In Dayton, it's the same thing—a little less. In Chicago
they would come and pinch me and ask me if I'm all right. I was
doing the work, but my eyes were in a daze, they said. I was in
Kentucky; that's where I was! I was in my dreams, my mountain
dreams."[3]

Hannah Morgan is no schizophrenic or religious escapist. She
has a healthy suspicion of easy pieties and knows quite well the
enemy that Betty Friedan fears and attacks. On the other hand,
she is also skeptical of approaches to life that would rob her of the
feelings she has for her mountain home, her family, her unique
perspective as an Appalachian woman. So it would not be enough,
for her, to deal with "Woman and the Workplace" and say virtually nothing about the inner life of those who labor at society's
thankless tasks.[4] As much as the Black people who fashioned the
spirituals and blues as ways of coping with hard times,[5] Hannah's
people have always reached within themselves and come up with
alternate visions, pointers to hope. To deny these traditional resources to working people or fail to factor them into one's economic
or political analyses is to miss half their reality. In addition, any
economic vision that is to do women's relational needs full justice
has to be more than simply economic. The 62-cent dollar has to

change, but not by making both sexes soulless calculators, heartless predators.

I think that the first approach to those most hurt by the current inhumanities of the workplace ought to be to ask how they see themselves, what *they* would like to have change. Some of the first answers, no doubt, would be crass. When people are scraping for dollars they find it hard to think about much else. But if one were to keep asking, a different voice might sound—a voice like that of one of the women Studs Terkel interviewed for his book *Working*: "I think most of us are looking for a calling, not a job. Most of us, like the assembly line worker, have jobs that are too small for our spirit. Jobs are not big enough for people."[6] A good summary of what feminist spirituality ought to target in the area of work would be making jobs big enough for people.

PEERS

I wish that the problem of making jobs big enough for people were confined to one sector of society, that we might target it clearly for intensive care. The reality, however, is that many people in well-paying jobs also feel cramped and compromised. Somewhere between well-paying jobs and jobs that lead to marginal economic status lie professional and goverment jobs like my own. Here the pay is enough to keep worries about food and shelter away, but not enough to raise children with much leeway. Nonetheless, the first therapy I would wish upon my peers would be a better realization of the spiritual potential their work situation offers. Many do appreciate this and work out an understanding of what they are doing that gives them great satisfaction. However, at least as many others seem to stay in the university only because they have gained tenure. Teaching gives them little joy, scholarship and writing are too demanding, so they set up as cafeteria critics, time-wasting politicians. Highly sensitive to their own rights, they seldom make the imaginative effort needed to grasp the rights or hopes of staff people and administrators. On a day by day basis, they are a great burden and block of inertia.

Administrators will come into focus in the next section, when I try to deal with power holding on the basis of power systems I know best. Here let me link my contemplation of my working peers with the previous section by focusing on their treatment of staff people. In the university, staff people are mainly secretaries, assistants, and clerks. They are at least 80-percent female and their perspective on higher education is largely an untold story. When I match what I hear from such women with what I hear from women in my classes who hold similar positions in other institutions (city government, hospitals, law offices, social work, etc.), "the underside of history" becomes an intriguing notion. I will fictionalize here, lest the knife cut too close to specific joints and marrows, but I will not falsify.

Once, in a school far away, I went to lunch with a secretary and a social worker. The secretary worked in pleasant surroundings on the twelfth floor of a humanities tower. Spread out before her lay a gorgeous bay and in the distance, foothills that on occasion were topped with snow. She had a wealth of office equipment: Xerox machine, memory typewriter, dictaphone, and the rest. Her pay was poor, and she had to park in a designated lot far from her office, but those were not her main grievances. Her main grievance was the thoughtlessness of the people for whom she worked. Their thoughtlessness showed in all the little things they might have considered but virtually never did. So, for instance, they seldom got their typing jobs to her except right on top of the deadline when the polished version was due. They seldom remembered to tell her when they would be out of town or not available to students. On weekends they would visit the office and work at her desk, leaving a mess of papers, pens, candy wrappers, and the like. If she did not leave the office during her lunch break they would ask her to do something in the middle of a sandwich. None of these things, she said, was of great moment individually. Together, however, they were a drag on her spirit, a wound to her pride. She wanted to do good work, neat work, work with some flair. Instead of helping her achieve this artistic goal, the people she worked for were her main obstacles.

The social worker had analogous stories to tell, mainly dealing with red tape and bureaucratic frustrations her job entailed. Sometimes she was able to accomplish a great deal, but more often her best sense of what ought to be done for an aged person, or an unwed mother, or a family on welfare ran afoul of procedures or the backlog of cases. In her profession burnout was a scar on every horizon. She felt herself growing a thick skin to shield her from the constant assaults on her sensitivity and idealism. Some loss of innocence, she knew, was good. Other losses she could have done without, for they were making her think she could do no more than hand out Bandaids. She was fortunate in having a few fellow workers who functioned as an informal support group, but on the whole she was feeling more and more put upon, underpaid and overloaded.

When the women asked me what I experienced as a professor, I had to say that my lot seemed easier. I was not directly harassed and I had considerable job satisfaction. Still, I could find many parallels to their situations, especially when I thought of how the going educational system remained tilted sexually. At the time of our conversation the big news on the sports pages was a controversy over the disparities between the expenditures for men's athletic programs and the expenditures for women's. This was not a battle close to my interests, but it had alerted me to a dimension of university life I hadn't previously appreciated. The big threat in changing over to a more equitable system, the defenders of the status quo said, was a loss of alumni support and TV revenue. If the school's football and basketball teams weren't big winners, the alumni would raise hell. I had thought this was exaggerated until I moved to the middle of the country and heard about the football scene at Nebraska, Oklahoma, and Texas. A lot of macho sickness there. In some cases, real pathology.

The sexism in strictly academic matters, I found, was less grotesque but still a constant cloud. Men were always sniping at our women's studies program; I had watched several female administrators get passed over for promotions they deserved, and the higher I mounted the ladder of rank the fewer women I found on the choice committees and in the inner sanctums. There, at the university's supposed heart, the accepted mental model was almost crudely empiricist, quite openly antagonistic to feminist notions of care, relationship, or holism. There, for the first time, I wondered whether an alert woman could call a full professor her peer.

BOSSES

I have been a peer in situations supposedly even more idealistic than the university (religious life), so I know that true colleagueship is rare and hard won. I have been a boss in a small way (departmental chair), so I know that my peers in the professorate are often no less inconsiderate toward their superiors than they are toward their supporting staff. Both "up" and "down," they can show a cretinous lack of imagination. In the case of my bossdom things seemed compounded by a syndrome of "Let Big Mother (5' 3") Do It," but I am sure that an egregious lack of imagination can adapt quite well to variations in sex, size, age, and the rest. After men have spent overlong periods in short pants, any authority figure is going to attract considerable wrath. So I sympathize with administrative superiors and grant them large drafts of credit. It is all the more distressing, therefore, to find again and again that they overdraw my good will and are now bankrupt in credibility.

At that same university by the coast, long ago, the administrative center went by the name "the black hole." Send anything toward it and the thing vanished, pulled by some primeval force to a place where the sun didn't shine. Since the men in charge of this administrative center were not stupid, I hypothesized that there was some method in their darkness. And, indeed, when I described the situation to a group of administrators at a meeting of the Society for Values in Higher Education, the verdict was, "Wily bastards!" In the view of their peers, our administrators had to be more deliberate than bumbling, and were sure bets to have worked out in clear advertence their policies of delay and distraction. What surprised me, however, was the tone of admiration that rang in the rendering of this verdict. Apparently having to brave the wars of complex institutions makes even idealistic bosses liable to amnesia, forgetting why people form communities in the first place.

To my mind, it is the sheerest of follies to conceive of leadership as simply keeping the ship afloat, putting out the fires in the engine room or making sure the flag still flies. Certainly any institution dedicated to spiritual ideals and goals, such as a school or a church, is badly served if not crippled by such a notion of leadership. Such institutions only flourish when at least a solid majority of the members contribute their talents and services with enthusiasm. Give out the message that innovation will be rare, imagination is not welcome, committee work will be mainly a waste of time and you will demoralize your best and brightest, bring the gun to your institution's head. This seems to me so obvious that I blush to lay it before anyone of sound mind and thirty years of age. Why, then, is there so much inertia and stagnation in our schools and religious bodies? What is the cause of the "black-holedom," the apparent will to suicide?

I am not a social psychologist, and I have already made my allusions to original sin, so here I shall have to settle for some common sense. Putting aside fancy speculations, and trying just to see things as they really are, I have come to a very simple conclusion. The cause is the mediocrity of our leadership, their lack of distinction in brains and guts. I do not mean that they have no brains or guts. They can be shrewd indeed in matters of survival, capable of braving a good many hassles. But there is little distinction in them, and so little joy among the workers they should lead. Leadership demands imagination, a touch of charisma, the ability to inspire people to bring forward their best. It demands such apparently humble but actually rare qualities as doing what one says one will do (when one says one will do it), keeping people informed, playing fair, crossing the line between professional relationships and friendships nimbly. Without these, jobs will continue to be too small for people.

On the whole, I find women better candidates than men for distinguished administrative leadership in institutions directly concerned with the human spirit. The personal debts that one assumes on entering into a working relationship with another person tend to weigh heavier on women than on men: the responsibility to keep the other person apprised, the obligation to remember how thoughtfulness greases gears. I find my female collaborators, by and large, more gifted at working with others, conceiving tasks as communal projects, and contributing to discussions and analyses constructively, in ways that build bridges and get everyone's involvement. Certainly I have known women who were inefficient and obnoxious, but that has not been the rule. The care that Gilligan documents as clearly present in girls by the age of eight tends to mean that women are almost scrupulous about details that affect concrete people's welfare. Given half a measure of support, the female administrators I have observed spend themselves prodigally to make their group a happy collective and their office a good place to work. I know that I shed blood, sweat, and tears for the group that I was in charge of, and the lack of response from that group was a major reason I reconsidered a career in administration.

Will there be bosses in the Kingdom to come? I'm not sure. When the lion lies down with the lamb, a whole new order will obtain. Still, I don't immediately see any objection to having a division of labor in one's utopia. If it is honest and open, what is the problem with a scheme that places some people in charge of others, parcels out bigger responsibilities to some and smaller to others? Unless we are all to be clones, we shall continue to differ from one another in brightness, as star differs from star. What I do know is that the noxious potential in "superior" and "inferior" shall have fled, for after the parousia we shall all know one another much better, all see much better the sort of work the other ought to have.

MONEY

To many people money is the main counter for work, the blue chip that sums work up. I used to think that this was so crude an outlook as to be beneath contempt, but in recent years I have had to become more sophisticated. I still believe that money is not the core of work and something relatively peripheral, but the seeming increase of greed in our society, the fawning over and gilding of the rich combined with the (related) increase of disdain for those badly off, makes me look again at money's ties to the penitential aspect of work, our sad need to earn our bread by the sweat of our brow.

First, it now seems to me clear that a society or economic system that does not make the provision of necessities to all its people the first priority deserves disrespect and discredit from Christians and all others committed to careful love. Second, the bottom line regarding money and all other aspects of economics and politics now seems to me just what it has always been in an authentic Christian view of social justice: No one has the right to superfluities so long as anyone lacks necessities. Thus to reach the point where some people in the world loaf and rake in millions while others toil from dawn to dusk for a pittance is to disclose the brutal twistedness of human work, the dark collusion of money and evil. If money is not the root of all evils (closure to God seems a better candidate), it certainly is right down there in the muck.

For my female students, who generally run from upper-lower to middle-middle class, money is mostly a worry. Few of them have sufficient financial resources yet to give money no thought, let alone be lavish and wasteful. The first item on their career agendas is securing a house, car, and education for their kids. So it was typical that a woman in my class whose arm had gone numb, and who showed other symptoms of a stroke, would beg me to take her to the hospital by car, rather than call an ambulance, because the ambulance would put a big dent in her family's budget. From time to time we get wealthy ladies, but my class is usually a jeans-and-sweater crowd. They have come to school to try to improve their job prospects. This makes it hard to teach them the humanities, until they start to realize that the evils of their society are not accidental. When the 62-cent female dollar starts to relate to sexism and economic injustice, and then sexism and injustice start to stand for disordered personalities, and then disordered personalities connect with idolatry, one has made nexuses that can take students far beyond crude pragmatism. I only hope to make it impossible for them ever to go back to that conceptual sty again. (I realize, however, this is not a completely kind ambition. The sty has a lot of warm bodies.)

Still, I fear for my students in "Women and Religion," because so much in our society supports crude pragmatism, laissez-faire economics, making it at any price. On the front page are the president and the first lady, flying off to their ranch in heaven. On the inside page the gossip-fashion columnist is making another fast pitch for trash. And so it goes in the other mass media. From this side and that, my students are under assault: "Buy me, I give pleasure. Wear me, I'll make you sexy. Look chic—it doesn't get any better." I think the students know that these are false sirens. In their bones, I think, they realize that if it doesn't get any better than tight-bottomed jeans and goppy mascara, it's hell, pure and endless. But many of them seem like lambs before the slaughterer, so ill-defended by their education and religion that their blood is nearly sure to run. Their way to wisdom seems certain to pass through considerable suffering, as Aeschylus and most other tragedians would have forecast. So I find myself becoming resigned. If my students will only come to themselves when they've chewed on the husks, gotten down and groveled in the tawdry, so be it. When the way down proves to have led to the way up, God again becomes providential. Still, it seems such a waste of beauty and potential, so cruel a kind of growth.

Money, then, is in my thoughts quite often. If I accept my society's rather blatant notion that you are what you earn, I am not very much. For consolation I think of Paul's words to Corinthians: "For consider your call, brethren; not many of you were wise according to worldly standards, not many were powerful, not many were of noble birth; but God chose what is foolish in the world to shame the wise, God chose what is weak in the world to shame the strong, God chose what is low and despised in the world, even things that are not, to bring to nothing things that are . . ." (I Corinthians 1:26–28). To buttress this I go back to the beatitudes: "Blessed are the poor in spirit, for theirs is the kingdom of heaven . . . Blessed are the pure in heart, for they shall see God" (Matthew 5:3,8).

These evangelical sayings judge me just as harshly as the false standards of my affluent, worldly society, but at least in them there is a breath of life, righteousness, the chance to become more human. The write-off I get from the wealthy people in my community, those who are a big success, has nothing redemptive about it. Whether I succeed or fail by their standards, I am left a spiritual shell. So I'd rather be castigated for missing the biblical poverty, not having the guts and wit to be stripped, than for missing the marks of fur and paté.

Consequently, this is what I try to teach: Money is necessary but dangerous. If you don't have enough to live simply and spiritually, with access to the cultural goods that most make you human, you must hustle. When you have more than what is necessary for such a spare spirituality, you must come before your God regularly in fear and trembling, lest you be losing your soul. This night your soul may be required of you. Your barns and designer racks will not avail. So store up treasures of learning and service. Find yourself work for which you need not blush.

LIBERTY

The children of God ought to be free of demoniac money. My little sisters ought to aspire to a work that will make them whole. When they seem to be expanding their lungs, taking deep draughts of liberty, I think of Augustine: Love and do what you will. One of the good things about our historical period is the new freedom women have to think of their work as a medium for their growth. In my geographical area, for instance, there has recently been a flowering of women artists, some doing exquisite work. Perhaps their talent and drive are such that they would have prospered in any time, but somehow I doubt it. It seems to me that they are benefitting from a lot of hard work and suffering that pioneer predecessors went through, and the most mature of them acknowledge as much. The less mature, who don't realize what doors have opened, seem either to assume that justice occurs naturally or to gripe about the distance still separating us from utopia. Sometimes this difference breaks down along generational lines, the older women in my classes pointing out that progress only comes by relentless work and the younger not quite knowing what the older mean.

My own seizure of liberty has been slow but steady. I am far from having arrived, but I see more clearly some of the main psychodynamics of the process. The one that strikes me most forcefully now is the need to discipline my desire for relationship. Having been brought up to care, to prize holism and relationship, I have been hurt when it hasn't occurred, when my working situation (dominated by males) hasn't valued it. More precisely, I have been hurt when I have put forward special quantities of work, generosity, and loyalty, only to find them making no dent, being shunted back to me with the label, "unappreciated." This still stops me like the surd of sin, and I still wonder about the tactic that seems my most logical self-defense. But, right now, I'm exploring this tactic.

The tactic is, bluntly put, not to give a damn what others think or whether others reciprocate. More subtly, it is to make more distinctions in my desire for relationship, place more refinements on my desire to be liked. Relationship, obviously enough, is a two-way street. I have yet fully to accept the fact that I can't effect it alone. It seems to me so obvious that one returns calls, answers mail, tries one's damndest to fulfill commitments that I still stagger when others don't concur. Of course, most others do concur on the level of discussion. But on the level of deeds, the slant that really matters, a very large number don't pull their load. The same in terms of emotional exchanges. The number of people willing to hold up their end of a friendship, do the deeds and show the care, is enough to keep the notion of Christ's Body viable, but hardly enough to make one confuse the university or the church with the host of heaven. And, sorest of all, the number of students in my school who do their work without being pressured by deadlines and threats is perhaps 15 percent. Since teaching, too, is a two-way street, a relationship and communication process, what I have been trying to get clear about colleagueship has sharp-cutting analogues in my work in the classroom.

Actually, the analogical relationship now seems to be moving the other way, from what I have learned about dealing with students to what I should do in trying to handle my unreceptive peers. There are some differences, in that I both have more control over my students and have received more positive feedback from them, but much in the parallelism holds. What I have learned from dealing with the students goes, in religious terms, by the name "detachment." I now worry the relationship less, invest less in things out of my control, such as students' willingness to do their work. I try to make the work interesting, program in enough tests and constraints to entice those who are not self-starters, and then I say to hell with it. I'm not God, and I'm not going to become a policewoman. If students don't get what they might have after I've made reasonable efforts and guidelines, the loss of time and money is on them and their descendents.

The hermeneutics of suspicion being rampant, I probably have to add the information that I am, by the quite dubious criteria of our student evaluations, a very successful teacher—90th percentile, winner of the college's teaching award. So the sobriety or even jaundice in my realism is not a cover for a bad performance or a bad press. It is also not my dominant mood: I still go 65 percent of the way toward students in the teacher-student relationship, and I still find more than enough who do their share to make this work extremely fulfilling.

With my colleagues, where the focus of work is more diffuse and emotions run high, the sobriety may be more necessary, a shield I can less easily do without. For the liberty of this child of God seems to mean finding a way not to care that a disgruntled little Yankee won't talk to me, a dipsomaniacal old boy tries to hack up my work. It is not good form, types such as these have told me, to publish a passel of books. Even when one is candid with oneself about the goal of such books, and equally candid with others, it inflames the green-eyed toads. I now know better what Chuang Tzu meant when he counseled anonymity, staying far from the reward-halls of court. That would give the small people less cause to become upset, the insecure less reason to soil themselves. Still, I note that Chuang Tzu kept writing and that he paid little heed to Confucian *amour propre*. Where the Confucians were prickly about status, he couldn't have cared less. And I notice that Jesus was a free spirit who accepted the inevitability of offending some. He piped them a song and they would not dance. He played them a dirge and they would not mourn. I'm trying to gain a like liberty, mainly by letting go.

CARE

Does this push toward liberty mean you're witnessing a formidable toughening up process? I rather doubt it. I find the games university people play too exhausting, the cabals too seldom worth it. And, more interiorly, care and vulnerability are too central to my self-conception. I could not lose them without losing myself. It is a balance I'm looking for, a better way to handle the tears. I see so many good things that I instinctively think could easily be, certainly ought to be, and I rush forward to make them, only realizing once I've exposed myself that others are far from agreed. The alternative to this window of vulnerability doesn't seem to be closing up, going frigid like one of the boys. It seems, for me, to be sallying forth with little to lose, letting my chips fall where they may. I want to keep caring, imagining, promoting, but without suffering such a toll. I believe every bit as much as I ever did that kindness and cooperation are godly. When the ungodly insist on other rules the solution is not to be converted to their rules. The solution is to keep playing by my own rules, but with a deeper faith, a care that is more carefree.

Which means, of course, that I must develop distinctions in my care to parallel those in my desire for relationship, my need to be liked. There is a care that is excessive, neurotic, a not-so-subtle playing of God. Oppressive mothers display it, the types that are always on you. Instructively, many of them are also hypersensitive, which merely doubles the bind. They make it hard when told to back off, so quick are their tears and sulks. I don't really think I have been relating to my colleagues that way, but I want to read from the type a strong word of caution. As the mother would care better by caring less, loving in more carefree (faithful, believing, religious) fashion, so often might I. I plant, others water, but only God gives the increase. If I plant well, I can care less what grows. Should God not want my carelessness, the new pose I am proposing, she's quite capable of letting me know.

Granted this distinction, however, I hope to continue to care for my work and those it contacts. In teaching, certainly, one of the intangibles that makes a course go is the students' liking the teacher. Often I think that if the teacher can win the students' sympathy, get them on her side, she has pretty much won the war. And how does a teacher do this? What is the capital trick? It is realizing that there is no trick: the way to being liked is being likable—intelligent, interesting, competent, sympathetic, humorous, and all the rest. In the classroom I know that this will not always carry, some students will turn me off. But over twenty-five years I've had enough success to make such knowledge nothing fearsome, just a memo from reality. Almost always I can use my authority in the classroom, my mandate to control, to bring about a multi-directional flow of good feelings, a group that by the end is a circle of friends. When one is working in a circle of friends, time flies and good things happen. When the circle focuses on learning, has an intellectual hub, the good things include the stimulus of the imagination, the firing of the active intellect, the openness of the passive intellect, and the procession of words that breathe forth love.

The last sentence puts the work of the classroom into imagery from scholastic epistemology. That is the sort of game I learned to enjoy back when I was doing philosophy. Other games for other kinds of work, the translator in me now says: How can we make other working conditions more amenable to becoming cooperative circles of friendship, conjoint ventures in loving what we're doing, enjoying the ride as much as the arrival? Probably by extrapolating the point about liking, and underscoring the freedom from concern that must accompany any effort to get oneself liked-into-leverage (open people to one's influence, gain the benefit of their doubt). As long as we don't worry overmuch about failing, we should act the way we want others to act and make believe we have a good working situation. I know that this effort can be very hard, and I want to insist that one *ought* to find such an effort supported, even applauded. But with or without support, I'm now trying to convince myself, we should do it: offer the hand, let fly the quip, assume that the other may come out of his rigor and rise up from the dead.

For faith, this is but a roundabout way of coming to witness and testimony, being not just a proclaimer of the word but a doer. If everything is ours, because we are Christ's and Christ is God's, then we can have confidence on any day of judgment by our peers. It does not matter that our peers may not share this foundation. It would be better if they did, but whether they do or not is out of our control. What matters is what is within our control: our own resting upon, relying upon, this foundation. For freedom this foundation, the keystone which is Christ, has set me free. Resting upon it I am free to care, free to love, free to be vulnerable, and free to set limits to how much flak I shall take. If the Spirit wills that I take a lot of flak, make up in my body and psyche some of the sufferings wanting to the Body of Christ, so be it. She will make herself clear. Until she has settled the issue, however, I am free. That is my birthright. That is my strength. People who don't want us free wouldn't have been very good friends anyway. People who care about freedom, help us to enhance it, rejoice in what it can bring them, may be the other half of our soul, the true friend we're always seeking, at work and everywhere else.

7   *FAMILY LIFE*

MARITAL FRIENDSHIP

The family life that I shall be discussing circles around a marital compact. At the heart of such a compact, at least ideally, is a friendship like that for which we are already searching, a bond that gives us the other half of our soul. Implicit in this very old characterization of a friend (*dimidium animae meae*) is a very new appreciation of relationship. If another is (holds) the other half of my soul, then certainly I can only be my full self by joining with that other. In a few cases the other may be God, the friend on the end of the line of celibacy or consecrated virginity. For those who have such a charism, the friendship of God is a great risk, a daring adventure, and quite an heroic business. People questing for God in this way can of course have human friends, sometimes very intimate and precious. But their gamble is not the partnership of two people trying to become a single flesh, two whole psycho-somatic units trying to combine into something considerably more than the sum of themselves as parts. It is this second venture that I am spotlighting, the conjunction of marital opposites.

If the marital friend is the other half of one's soul, he or she is also the other half of one's Platonic *Urmensch*, that round, eight-limbed creature discussed in the *Symposium*. When the boys sat down to toss a few back and started making myth about human origins, among their draggings from the deep was a picture of original humanity as androgynous. Somehow the original androgyne got split up into a female and male component. Ever since, the two components have been longing to be reunited, which explains the explosive power of eros. This eros (the only thing in which Socrates claims expertise) is a far cry from the bogey that sends people into erotic movies. It is a noble love, a lifting of mind, heart, soul, and strength. One of Christianity's biggest historical failings has been its inability to appreciate the platonic eros and see its kinship with the eternal life of God.

The friendship of marriage combines eros and *philia.* Philia is the common mind (*homonoia*) that makes friends compatible intellectually, sharers of a similar vision. Certainly part of what marital partners crave is this similarity of vision. When their craving is fulfilled and patterned with their fascination over how differently the vision can be embodied, they have the wonder that is the beginning of a long voyage of discovery. In the first years the discovery is likely to proceed by face to face explorations. In later years it is apt to position the two side by side. Combined, the two postures give the couple a rich life, whether they are looking across the table at one another or confronting the world as allies. The mid-world of their face to face intimacy has a microcosmic beguilement. The larger cosmos into which they stride with arms locked keeps them realistic and humble. It is a good way to live, for it actualizes two very basic biblical precepts. The first is that in the beginning God made humanity male and female, a conjoint image. The second is that it is not good for human beings to be alone.

So much for a few marital basics. What now about the optional part of the program, the diverse ways that spouses can enact their friendship and support one another's spirituality? It seems to me that whenever two people can agree that they are a cooperative, a combine, they make it possible to mow down much of the opposition. In the case of spirituality, the opposition without is the large band of fellow workers and neighbors who apparently know little about Christian spirituality, and apparently care even less. The opposition within is the discouragement and loneliness this outside indifference can foster. A spouse helped by a spouse is like a strong city well protected against such opposition. If the one person to whom I am most deeply committed, with whom my fate is being forged, agrees with me about what is really important and wants the same foundational stone, most of the opposition will dissolve into mist.

The heart of the matter, then, is an eros and philia that make spouses strong in their convictions, able to make a stand in their public worlds. The other organs of the matter include agreements about how resources will be spent (time even more than money), how obligations (to children, friends, jobs, housework) will be met, how the couple will play and recreate, what prayer is going to mean, how politics is going to factor in, and so forth. It is better when these agreements are explicit, but even implicit agreements will do. The point is giving and receiving the support, challenge, complementarity and the like necessary for a whole life, a spirituality alive, realistic, and round.[1]

So, for example, when I sail out to the academic wars knowing that I have my husband's full support, his full complement of advice-agreement-love-respect-admiration-pride, I am much more confident and carefree than I would be were I alone, or were I married to someone who did not agree with what I am doing. Saint Teresa felt that she and God were a majority. She was much closer to God than I. I am able, though, to make do with my husband's and my being a majority. This is not, we hope, an exclusion of God's contribution nor an under-appreciation, but an effort to fulfill our mandate to become identified, unified, possessed of a single flesh.[2] When our sexual union produces such a spiritual solidarity that we can handle all but the worst slings and arrows, we know that our friendship is in very good shape.

SEXUAL LOVE

Sexual intercourse is the act most symbolic of marriage, the sacrament of the marital sacrament. The freedom with which we enjoy sexual intercourse and the care in its love have a major say in the pleasure and prospering of our whole family life. Certainly good sexual love is not the only necessity for a good marriage. It is, however, an enormous boost, nourishment, and source of energy. My own Roman Catholic tradition has noticeably been struggling with this question recently, filling the newspapers with Vatican statements and the faithful's several shadings of demur. One of the best recent reflections on the marital relationship, written by two Catholic married women, a psychiatrist and a theologian, makes much of the importance of sexual attraction as a key role in the happy beginnings.[3] The more official pronouncers probably would not have great trouble with this perspective, unless it somehow ran afoul of the established positions on birth control. When one sees how the present pope tends to think about sexual intercourse, such running afoul is not hard to picture.

In doing research for an article on Roman Catholic views of marriage[4] I came across the following passage written by Karol Wojtyla before he became Pope John Paul II:

> Mechanical means [of contraception] cause local injuries in the woman's reproductive tract, and what is more interfere with the spontaneity of the sexual act, which is something that women in particular find intolerable. Perhaps the most frequent method used by married couples is the *coitus interruptus*, which they resort to thoughtlessly, without realizing at the time that it must inevitably have undesirable consequences. Ignoring for the moment the fallibility of this method of preventing fertilization, let us ask ourselves why people resort to it. At first glance, it may seem that the egoism of the male is the sole cause of this behavior. Deeper analysis, however, reveals that in interrupting the sexual act the male often supposes that he is doing so to 'protect' the woman. It is indeed true that when a man does this the woman is robbed of various goods—she is denied orgasm, her nervous equilibrium is upset, but her basic capacity, her fertility, is unaffected. For this reason women themselves are often convinced that 'it doesn't do any harm.' For his part, the man feels that he is in control of the situation, that he is making the decision. While the woman maintains the attitude of sexual passivity that is proper to her and leaves the responsibility to the man.[5]

It may be that more recently the pope has changed his view,[6] or found a more skillful translator, but passages such as this will give feminists good reason to take a very skeptical look. When I read this passage to my class on "Women and Religion" the reaction was strong and unified: What right does this man have to speak for women's sexual experience? On deeper analysis, the passage becomes only more objectionable. It is possible to interpret it as blaming the woman for *coitus interruptus*, as saying that a woman's basic capacity is her womb, and as proposing that women's proper sexual attitude is to be passive, even irresponsible.

With chasms like that to cross, there's not much point in trying to shout replies. Feminists would need an alpine horn, or a majority of seats in the cardinalate. Better that they should listen peacefully and then love and do what they will. Better that their helical progress not flag, and neither their drive nor their care lessen. Good sexual love is not something encoded biologically. It is not etched in our natures as a set of laws we cannot fail to find. The great merit in the pope's approach to morality has been his application of phenomenological methods that give greater personal nuance than the old metaphysical approaches of the scholastic theories of natural law. But he comes a cropper when he tries to imagine the atmosphere of spousal love-making, and one wonders what hubris ever caused him to try.

Sexual love is connected to procreation, of course, and in the next three sections I shall ponder the fruits of this connection. It is a good in its own right, however, and one that both contemporary personalism and contemporary population pressures have tended to make primary. The end (*finis*: goal) of marriage today cannot be procreation conceived as it was when the classical Catholic theologians, following the lead of Augustine, made *proles* (children) the first end of the marital relationship. It has to be generativity in the larger sense that developmental psychologists such as Erik Erikson have brought out: fruitfulness in all its possible forms. When it is, the conception of marriage as a consecrated mode of self-transcendence comes into a bold and clear relief.

Two people make love, and share their whole lives, in order to become more and more fruitful. If they accept the biblical criterion that by their fruits they shall be known, they strive for a friendship, parenthood, set of careers, neighborliness and the like that will be productive: Make things of beauty and utility, things worthy of the Creator in whose image they work and love. The mutual help that the tradition made the second end of marriage is not an end at all; it is a constant modality or means. In bed the couple help one another relax, heal, take fire, enjoy, and experience that what God has made is very good. With the kids they help one another wonder, protect, nourish, endure, let free, worry, and admire. In work they cooperate, collaborate, conspire, fill in for one another, criticize, endure, create, grow more carefree. In as many things as they can, they work for good with the one who loves them, the one called according to God's purpose to be the other half of their soul.

CHILDREN

When mutual help is the basic modality of a marriage, a family can grow up on a basis of equality. When mutual help is not forthcoming, and one spouse is subordinate to the other, a family is almost sure to develop asymmetrically, almost fated to become ugly or queer. For some time I have been reading the novels of Anne Tyler as a laboratory of family life. Again and again she creates queer families peopled by eccentrics, and I have started to correlate this (very funny) craziness with the spouses' lack of sexual equality and drama. Insofar as we are allowed to know them, these peculiar men and women have few erotic interactions as equals. Children abound, runny at the nose and cranky at the voicebox, but a mutual help to passion, intense communication, orgasmic joy is rare if not invisible. So, for all their wit and sociological insight, the novels read like descriptions of a culture that owes no debt to Provençe, careens on its way untouched by romance, eros, ardor. Tyler gives hints that she is aware of the connections between the sorts of households she depicts and the main characters' lack of passionate sexual communication, but they are not enough to be conclusive.

Consider the following description of the separation of Daniel and Margaret Rose, two characters in *Searching for Caleb*: "They had six children. In 1905 Justin II was born, in 1906 Sarah, in 1907 Daniel Jr., in 1908 Marcus, in 1909 Laura May, in 1910 Caroline. In 1911, Margaret Rose left home. She had wanted to take the children to Washington on the train for her mother's birthday. Daniel didn't think she ought to. After all, she was a Peck now. What did she want with the Bells? Who at any rate were an undisciplined, frivolous, giggling lot. She said she would go anyway. Daniel pointed out that she was her own mistress, certainly, as everyone in his family had noticed more than once, but the children were *his* . . . . She could go, Daniel said, but she couldn't take the children. And he expected her back on Saturday evening as there was church to attend Sunday morning. She went. Saturday evening Caleb met the train but Margaret was not on it. When Daniel found out he merely pressed his lips together and walked away."[7]

Daniel seems to be small loss to Margaret Rose, and not just because Margaret seems to be small loss to Daniel. She has been portrayed as lively, happy, affectionate, and he has progressively become the stereotypical lawyer, a man dominated by a narrow mind. So we glimpse, in a scene that precedes this rupture, the deep well of experience from which Margaret drew her decision to stay with her family, her definitive interpretation of Daniel's insufferable patriarchalism: "Meanwhile Daniel's house was filling up with children, and his practice was swelling, and he already had it in the back of his mind to become a judge someday while his sons carried on with the law firm. When he came home evenings, and Margaret ran up in her rustling, flowery dress to fling her arms around him, he would be remote and sometimes annoyed. His head was still crowded with torts and claims and statutes. He would set her gently aside and continue toward his study at the rear of the house. So for someone to talk to, Margaret tried giving afternoon tea parties."[8]

Clearly, Margaret and Daniel do not have a marital friendship, the love of philia. She cannot even get conversation out of him. Clearly (the six kids), they had some sex. It is tempting to think that their procreative success with sex (by Tyler's figures Margaret was pregnant 75 percent of the time, on average, from 1905–1910) was the reason she walked out in 1911, but that is not how the novel sets things up. The novel focuses on Daniel's coldness and arrogance, which culminate in his astounding claim that the children are his (alone). (I find Margaret's acquiescence to this claim incredible, although in 1911 it may well not have been.) What it leaves unsaid is the sort of sexual love that went into the making of those six children. We could infer that it likely was very unsatisfying to Margaret, except that she remains affectionate, warmly welcoming Daniel home. For reasons better than prurience, I think, we want to know how it was between Daniel and Margaret in times of intimacy—not the physical scenes so much as the emotional exchanges or blocks. To today's mind, children are the issue of an interaction that may be casual, brutal, ecstatic, or sanctifying. They become entities and values independent of this origin, and separable from its quality, but they never lose their potential to signalize a family's center in an amazingly complementary and fruitful love.

This is one of the first ties I would make between children and a spirituality conceived as self-transcendence. A couple's creation of new human life immediately takes them beyond, out into a new dimension of relationship (both to one another and to God). The wonder of the new life is in part the wonder that this happened to us. We did this—scrawny, no-account we. We created such a marvel. God be praised! Now we are responsible for its health, safety, happiness. God help us! So one tends to see on the faces of new parents strange little squints. They are peering at one another as well as the child, trying to get a whole new situation into focus. They have cooperated to make this prodigy, and this prodigy will only require more cooperation from them in the future.

So, they have to move beyond where they used to dwell, find new modes of freedom and new resources of love. God the giver of life has to become God the granter of freedom to make mistakes even in such important matters as childrearing. The Spirit who broods careful love at our depths has to turn pumping hormones and social applause into consolations that are spiritual, peace and joy that give confidence for the days ahead. It *is* possible to raise a child, all the newspaper columns (of advice, as well as crime) notwithstanding. It is right and just, fitting and helpful to salvation. When little Jessica or John Michael grins, no sane person could ever doubt it. Grin, Jessica, grin.

TEENAGERS

By the time that Jessica and John Michael have become teenagers, their parents have had considerable experience of their sign-quality. They have several times been a cause of alarm or a cause of comfort, and overall they have shown how one and one can make three or three-and-a-half. Because having children is quite ordinary in our society, as it has been quite ordinary throughout human history, we can miss the extraordinary pushes and pulls that children exert. People who would not put themselves out for the King of Siam will go down on their knees to try to comfort a toddler. People grown cynical from cruel handling will find themselves heartsick at a child's vulnerability. And all of this is growth, a progressive pilgrimage.[9] Old conceptions of self-concern and career-making suffer the assaults of kids' disingenuous appeals for help, entertainment, and love so that they soon seem narrow, immature, naive, and passé. A child somehow knows that it ought to be able to rely on its parents completely, and the parents somehow know that providing this reliability is a responsibility of mortal consequence, one of the few truly grave ethical obligations they shall face. To bring new life into the world and not to care for it, spend oneself for it, be willing to cut off an arm rather than knowingly damage it is, by both instinctive intuition and highly studied analysis, a most grievous default.

By the time that children enter the teenage years most parents have been sorely tempted to default several times. In the teenage years one is dealing with a body that is across the border into maturity and a mind that is God only knows where. Mediating between these two is a set of emotions that jump back and forth between maturity and childhood like frenzied rabbits. Perhaps the best way to sympathize with one's teenage kids is to focus on this emotional volatility, trying to recall what it was like to be fifteen, and trying to reflect very carefully on how one's present interactions with a problem-teen are going. Recurring to Anne Tyler again, I find myself realizing that some of her most memorable parents seem to lack both the ability to recall their own teenage years and the habit of reflecting on their present behavior toward their kids.

Pearl Tull, the central figure in *Dinner at the Homesick Restaurant,* is one of those memorable parents, and her lack of memory and reflection lead to a lack of sympathy that causes her to become quite violent, capable of outbursts that scar her children badly. The oldest child, Cody, is fourteen when this scene occurs. Just prior to it Pearl (whose husband has abandoned the family) has lit into Jenny, the youngest child: "She [Pearl] sat down serenely, as if finished with the subject forever, and reached for a bowl of peas. Jenny's face was streaming with tears, but she wasn't making a sound and Pearl seemed unaware of her. Cody cleared his throat. 'But that was Sunday,' he said. Pearl's serving spoon paused, midway between the bowl and her plate. She looked politely interested, 'Yes?' she said. 'This is Wednesday.' 'Yes.' 'It's Wednesday, dammit, it's three days later. So why bring up something from Sunday?' Pearl threw the spoon in his face. 'You upstart,' she said. She rose and slapped him across the cheek. 'You wretch, you ugly horror.' She grabbed one of Jenny's braids and yanked it so Jenny was pulled off her chair. 'Stupid clod,' she said to

Ezra [the middle child] and she took the bowl of peas and brought it down on his head. It didn't break, but peas flew everywhere. Ezra cowered, shielding his head with his arms. 'Parasites,' she told them. 'I wish you'd all die, and let me go free. I wish I'd find you dead in your beds.'"[10]

Pearl shows the volcanic side of family relations, the intense emotions that can erupt and pour forth like molten lava. We sympathize with her burden of three children, single parenthood long before it was respectable, working by day as a cashier and by night as a compulsive housekeeper. But we can't sympathize with this instability, this sick hatred. Her children have their faults, but on the whole they have adapted to their father's leaving and Pearl's bare household with considerable generosity. Pearl is a dry, correct woman on the surface, a woman greatly concerned with social forms. To find such violence under her surface is to realize that her society has badly malformed her, and that she colluded with this malformation, that she has never confronted what she has become and so never moved might and main to change.

All sorts of studies nowadays tell us that many American families suffer terrible violence. The stereotype focuses on the physically abusive husband and father, but the reality is more complex. There is also physical abuse by mothers and siblings, and emotional abuse all around. In the majority of cases, today's abusive parents are only handing on patterns, hurts, that they themselves received as children and teenagers. Cody, Jenny, and Ezra don't later treat children violently, but in real life there is a strong likelihood that they would. Looking at them as they sit around her table midway between childhood and adulthood, Pearl projects onto them the frustration, hurt, and anger she feels at more than forty years of unsuccessful living, forty years in which she has not become a person she likes, a person she accepts and loves.

Teenagers are especially vulnerable to the backlash of their parents' frustrations because in life-cycle terms they tend to confront their parents during the parents' midlife crises. The only way I can see to mediate the damnable irritations that teenagers create and parents' inner frustrations from career disappointments and the like is to be brutally honest, stringently reflective. If we can face up to our sins as parents, and honestly beg our teenage children's pardon, things usually will be redeemable.

YOUNG ADULTS

On the lips of Pearl Tull, "I beg your pardon" is but a bit of social amenity, or an implicit rebuke. One cannot imagine her saying this to her children with depth and sincerity. Her children are not independent people with inalienable rights to life, liberty, and an apology when she has abused them. They are much like Daniel Peck's children: possessions, things that one regards with pride or a sense of burden, depending upon whether they hone bright or dull.

Usually it takes a number of contests of will before children can become young adults, people recognized by their parents as at least semi-equals. I think that half the traumata that play through the revelations of patients to psychiatrists and counselors would vanish were parents to grant their children the respect, courtesy, and thoughtfulness that they try to grant their colleagues and friends. Conversely, if teenage children found themselves facing parental models of unremitting courtesy they would have much less excuse for rudeness and thoughtlessness. This would not eliminate their rudeness and thoughtlessness (it might, in the short run exacerbate them), but over the long haul it would make family life much easier.

God knows, I do not say this further to burden parents already heavily weighted down. There are times when restraint from violence, let along sweet courtesy, can be heroic virtue. One of the most sensible women I know, a teacher with psychiatric training, confessed to our liturgy group with equal parts of rue and humor that she had called the police the past week because she was afraid she would do bodily harm to her obnoxious teenage son. The woman knew that part of what she was confessing was her own failure to keep enough psychic strength in reserve to handle a crisis such as an outbreak of brattiness. She was trying to finish a degree, teach, compete in masters' swimming, and please a busy husband and quartet of kids. It was too much, even for a person of her strength, and to her credit she realized it.

To recognize the danger signals in family relations, it greatly helps to examine one's conscience daily, meditate reflectively in the ways I have sketched. When we do this, the main features of our psychic landscape are virtually unescapable. Whatever is irritating us is right there in view, as the sore to which we keep returning.

More subtly, also in view are the dangerous self-congratulations we have been indulging, the over-inflations of our egos. The over-inflations of their egos (for example, Pearl Tull's social pretensions) play see-saw with the depressions of manic-depressive parents, depriving their children of the consistency the children so greatly need.

The consolations of the Spirit are not over-inflating; they do not make us head for the ceiling like helium balloons. They take us in the direction of a sober peace and joy, a realistic humility and hope. And, in the case of troublesome offspring, they remind us that our responsibilities have limits. As the children age, we have to let go even of our anxieties and permit our children sufficient freedom to make mistakes. Otherwise, we become hindrances to their maturation, burdens rather than aids.

A major challenge facing feminists and other people of idealistic bent today is to guide children away from our society's materialism, sexism, and irreligion, to bring up young adults who want something more just and fulfilling.[11] In the relationship between mothers and daughters, which many women find especially troublesome, this sets a demanding agenda. During their teenage years girls are still subject to pressures that work at cross-purposes, and so they are still apt to feel torn apart. On the one hand, they are expected to be docile, good students, sweet and loyal. In matters of dress, speech, and behavior they are still subject to strong peer pressure. On the other hand, they are suppose to be a new generation with career possibilities equal to boys. They are supposed to be sufficiently aggressive and self-confident to fight for their rights. It is a big set of challenges and many girls seem overwhelmed by it. As a result, many mothers of teenage girls have to take heavy amounts of flak.

What I see on the college scene is a strong need for good direction. Fortunately, many schools now have good women's studies programs that offer formal or informal counseling. Usually the upshot of such counseling is patience: It takes time to put the new package together. My own urgings to female students are in part things I would tell any undergraduate and in part things I say because of the current sexual atmosphere. The common advice runs toward working out a double major. As a teacher in the humanities division, I am constantly faced with two sets of facts.

One is the dismal job prospects for people who have only a liberal arts background. The other is the dismal personal prospects for people who lack a liberal arts background. My solution, at least for the better students, is to urge a both/and. I think that students have to develop survival skills for the society we conjecture will be dawning in the year 2000, and I think that they have to develop survival skills for the society that has existed since the dawn of reflective consciousness: the society most beholden to the people who make art, music, literature, history, and religion, as ways to help us situate ourselves in a mysterious world.

The advice that targets today's special sexual atmosphere is nothing other than the spirituality I have been elaborating here. The helix of feminist growth has a side of freedom, pushing beyond present accomplishments, going onward and upward, and it has a side of loving care, responsive fidelity to the calls of the Creator to let go, the calls of the neighbor to help. Without both sides, in balance, a young woman is not likely to gain the growth for which she hopes, the known unknown burning within her.

GENERATIVITY

A family circle that sponsors the clarification and grasp of the known unknown burning within its young adults verifies a religious instinct like Pascal's: You would not seek God had you not already found God. As Lonergan, Rahner, and Voegelin all insist, we have present to us, by God's grace, the mysterious fulfillment on which our hearts have so long been set. The goal of our drive to know is nothing but the cause of the universe, the formality or mind that would make the whole intelligible. The goal of our passion to love is nothing but a good that would overspill the quasi-infinity of our capacity, something worthy of "whole mind, heart, soul, and strength." We are under way, on pilgrimage, ever restless because we have this heavenly spark in our secular clod. To try to estimate our proper generativity as either individuals or parents without reference to this heavenly spark, this call to the holy, is to denature the whole inquiry. That is why flat, two-dimensional sorts of humanism or secularism are bound to leave us hungry, irritated, unsatisfied. We have been made for more, and we can't deny this majority without denying the best that is in us, the most deeply demanding creativity and longing.

But, what can parents do to elucidate and elicit this sort of longing? How can their generativity infuse their work and children with a properly religious zeal? If they look to the right, they see a zeal that is repulsive, all sureness of concept and piety of tongue. If they look to the left they see wild chaos, longing that is denied, or let loose with no control, or attached to a different goal each semester. Is there no way to make the compact with Mystery efficient, productive, the heart and soul of a life that is balanced and uneccentric? Of course there is, although it is not easy.

The religious traditions, East and West, have laid out several variations on an approach, a "way," to wisdom and maturity. In Buddhist terms, the three areas it must integrate are meditation, wisdom, and morality. Meditation, broadly translated, is reflectiveness and the calming of the senses. By regular meditation one comes to know one's more-than-material needs and capacities, one's spirituality. Then the seductions of Madison Avenue and Wall Street become much less powerful. Then we have solid defense against all the invitations to waste our lives on crass pleasure, consumption, or power plays.

The person who meditates, who contemplates and examines her conscience daily, knows in her bones that most of the fashions and ideals set before her by the cultural mainstream are unworthy. She senses, though she may not be able to put it into words, that the "Post-Christianity" of her society more often than not means her society's trivialization. In the contemporary West, not to have Jesus' twofold commandment as the soul of culture has meant to shrink the soul of culture, and narrow the horizon of the best and the brightest. Certainly I could fashion a positive interpretation of the death of the God of nineteenth-century mainstream Christianity, but it would be more sophisticated than most situations in today's American society warrant. By and large, the unmeditative character of contemporary American society, coupled with its loss of its Christian moorings, means a culture careening toward nightmarish meaninglessness of arcade games and endless rock music.

Wisdom in the Buddhist scheme is the profound view of reality that enlightenment brings. Meditation is a main path to this wisdom, but study also helps. Failing personal experience of the *Praj-*

naparamita (the wisdom that leads to the other shore) through enlightenment, one can at least take to heart what the traditional masters and mistresses have taught. The *Prajnaparamita* is the Lady Wisdom who dwells beyond all the worldviews spawned by desire and illusion. It is what the bodhisattvas and buddhas, the beings who have realized the light at their core, see and live by. And it does not reside apart from daily life. The enlightened see it in the midst of daily life, as *nirvana* or perfection in the midst of *samsara*, the realm of dying and being reborn.[12]

Morality, the third leg of the tripod, is the practice, the living out of wisdom's vision. In the Buddhist scheme it runs by desirelessness and nonviolence. In the Christian scheme its heart is love. The five Buddhist precepts—not to kill, lie, steal, misuse sex, or drink intoxicants—have their counterpart in the Christian ten commandments. Both are but the framework for love of neighbor as self and proper regard for ultimate reality. Both should produce people mature in their interior lives and mature in their social behavior, their roles as citizens. Both have much to offer a profane spirituality of work and family living.

I think that the Christian churches have done their lay membership a major disservice by failing to challenge them to some simple yet profound regime like meditation, wisdom, and morality. The churches have seldom taught their people how to contemplate. They have been reluctant to offer the deep visions of the doctors and mystics. And they have not made clear the coincidence of morality with works of love. I don't say this in condemnation so much as regret. It is an awesome responsibility to lay out a hard, straight, deep path to maturity, and we should condole with churches as much as parents for having to bear it. On the other hand, we have a natural responsibility, an inbuilt need, to "tradition," to hand on, ideally by deepening, purifying, and personally embodying the best of what we ourselves have received. The bad news is that even our best efforts are only half a guarantee of success since our children remain free to accept or reject what we hand on. The good news is that if we live out a profound regime, and it manifestly gives our lives a helix of growth, our children will have lovely icons to cling to, even when we have long left them.

MENOPAUSE

At midlife the female body takes a pause and shifts toward a new mode of generativity. With the ceasing of one's capacity for physical fruitfulness, mental, spiritual, and political generativities can come into clearer perspective. Many women find this time very significant. Their children are leaving the nest and the second half of their life bids to be quite different than the first. When women at this stage appear in my classes, good things usually ensue. They have a wealth of experience to share with the younger students, and as soon as they get confidence in their voice they add depth and harmony to our chorus. In the best of cases they feel liberated, and this liberation makes them both witty and constructive critics. What they have to say about family life is often dazzlingly insightful, full of meaty suggestions for a feminist "traditioning." How might such a traditioning muse?

Beyond compulsion and necessity, the hormonal and economic forces that dominate the first half of life, there lies a vision of freedom and love that can sweeten the lives of many householders. Often the first import of such a transcendence is a greatly increased ability to say no. Patently, it is hard to say no to such powerful forces as the drive to unite, find climactic release, build a career, provide for one's young, and solidify a socio-individual self. The material goods advertised hither and yon lure most people forward in pursuit of "success," while the steamings of young adults' energies are like an internal combustion engine driving them from within. One tends to be swept along in the mainstream, only half aware of what farther shore is targeted. Until family life and career begin to settle, few of us reject the main powers molding our society. Regular reflection may lead a tiny bloc to become resistance fighters, but they tend to be a quiet minority while the majority let themselves be herded along with a discouraging bray.

Around the time of the menopause things can suddenly change. It appears that the kids are going to survive adolescence, that the bank is not going to snatch away the house, and that the career will turn out a modest success. It also appears that while the health or common sense of the mainstream one has followed deserves some respect, it in no way has proven worthy of worship. For women, especially, the penalties involved in following the mainstream have become more and more apparent. Indeed, women divorced at middle-age can find themselves financially and socially imperiled. Most of their work has gone into things not legally recognized. They have not had a contract stipulating the remunerations of midnight confortings, the fringe benefits of having put themselves last. They have been the soul of the household, its marrow and grace, yet in legal terms even their equality is suspect. If the male menopause should send their spouse after sleeker models, aging can fly at them like a vision of abandon. With one quick slap across the face, time's passing can show what a great deal they should have been saying no to.

Others can detail the legal aspects of this nay-saying, what feminist reforms of marital, financial, and labor law would entail. Sociologists and psychologists can sketch the reforms in mores. My province is religion, the domain of ultimate meaning, spirituality, and mystery. In my province the woman tossed by waves of mid-life crisis finds she should have been saying no to all the models of growth that did not provide for both sides of her helix. When society said that being female meant being sacrificial, caring for others to the neglect of herself, she should have been saying, "No, I too am a person. The foundation of altruistic love is the right love of oneself. Unless I too can unfold my wings, see new vistas, work out who I am through productive projects, the game is tilted and we all lose. God did not make me as second-rate image, a codicil or afterthought. In the beginning I was there as much as Adam. In the present so should it also be."

However, since the helix is double, like the genetic code, another side also calls for nay-saying. Where confused voices have suggested that a woman adopt macho ways, begin riding rough-shod, she finds that she should have been saying: "No, my care is also my self. I can no more deny gentleness, relationship, nurturing than I can deny my equal right to self-development. I wish that you male-driven society would outgrow your simple-mindedness and see the harmony of drive and caring, freedom and receptivity, yang and yin. Give over the false dichotomies you keep fashioning. Let go your enemy-making. People not against can be for you. Notice how seldom we women have dustups, punchouts, and bloody, destructive wars. How can you miss the obvious lesson, above all in a time of nuclear power? If you keep insisting you are the whole race, the race will go up in smoke."

With some such interior soliloquy or apostrophe, some such realization of all the denying that ought to have been, the woman at menopause can find herself radicalized. Going to the center of her embodied self, finding its ties to her inherited culture, and tracing these ties to their bedrock anchoring, she finds that much indeed has been lacking. So she is open to new possibilities, even old suggestions from her religious tradition. Perhaps, after all, life is a pilgrimage through a dark valley. Perhaps, despite its incarnationalism, historicism, and sacramentalism, Christianity is also otherworldly and passionately in love with a Wisdom that goes beyond.

ECCLESIOLAE

I don't see how we can have a church compatible with feminist truths without becoming passionately in love with a feminine Wisdom that goes beyond our current sexism. I don't see how we can have family units acceptable to both faith and feminist instinct without making Lady Wisdom the goddess of the house shrine. The family is the nuclear unit of society and the smallest form of the church. It should be an *ecclesiola*, a little gathering of people committed to Christ. When it is, the Freudian first pillar stands upright. The members are exchanging a love that guarantees them all a fair shot at happiness and maturity. Christ has died, Christ has risen, and Christ will come again and again to the little group that assembles in his name. True, many families find it hard to speak such a language at home, hard to ritualize the relationships that determine how they first think of themselves. I hope that future feminist spirituality will soften this hardship and make generous contributions to a domestic liturgy.

The liturgical image that comes to mind when I think of children being initiated into family prayer is the ritual of grace before meals. Often this is perfunctory, but on occasion it really does carry eucharistic overtones, a sense of thanksgiving for the cornucopia of God's gifts. Since such a sense is basic to the Christian understanding of grace (in the sense of God's saving love-life), the prayers before meals can be genuine sacramentals, signs of God's presence and love. If children not only pray to express their gratitude, but also recall the needy, the suffering, and those for whom no one cares, grace before dinner can become a vital connection to the rest of the world. As the children become old enough to understand simple reflections along this line, parents should try to make the grace a brief meditation. Even when the substance doesn't carry to the children, the form or habit may. At the least, it will lie among the inventory of possibilities in the child's memory should the need arise to give thanks, express concern, or deal with fear.

Most parents are not theologians and most have not been exposed to informal liturgies. Praying explicitly and publicly does not come easily to them. Thus they might find it more fruitful with teenagers to discuss religious issues in the context of current politics, economics, or the teenagers' social lives. A family can't be a small church if it does not provide some retreat from the thoughtlessness of the secular world. It has to try to supply a quiet, trust, and depth that help the young person handle the barrages being fired at her. How to accomplish this without seeming sententious or pious is a nice question. Still, I think too many parents worry about appearing affected, for often such worry only betrays the frailty of their own church-going.

In most households where parents love music or art, music and art flow unselfconsciously through the conversation, the recreation, the discussion of what counts. The same with sports or politics. Why should it be so different with God and religion? Why should basketball or scouting or making money be more natural, more legitimate, less in need of defense than Christ, God, the Spirit, prayer, or religious spurs to social justice? Only because the parents are not comfortable with such theological matters, and can't back up such words and notions with spontaneous convictions.

Parents caught in a bind between the religio-moral notions they profess on Sundays and the way they structure their households through the week are not likely to produce inward, religious children (except by way of revolt). In fact, they are likely to discourage their children's religious questions, since the questions quickly become embarrassing. So, for example, a couple of prosperous New Orleans parents felt it necessary to curb the questioning of their precociously reflective daughter. The daughter was brooding about the meaning of life in the wake of her grandmother's death. The black maid who interpreted the scene for Robert Coles stands in striking contrast to the parents:

"They're all right, these people here. I've worked for them for fifteen years. I'll stay with them, most likely, until they carry me out, and that'll be the end of things. My momma told me: remember that you're put here only for a few seconds of God's time, and He's testing you. He doesn't want answers, though. He wants you to know how to ask the right questions. If you learn how to do that, you'll do all right when you meet Him . . . These people here, they've got all that money, and all this big house, and another one out in the country, and still they won't let that little girl just be herself. She's eight or nine, and she's got an independent spirit in her, but they're determined to get rid of it, and they will, let me tell you, and soon. The girl asks me a lot of questions. That's good. She looks out on that cemetery and she starts to wondering about things. That's good. She wonders about life, and what it's about and what the end of things will be. That's good. But she's stopping now. That's what they want: no looking, no staring, no peeking at life. No questions; they don't want questions. They go to church a couple of times a year, Christmas and Easter, and no one asks them questions there. No one asks them questions anyplace they go."[13]

Once in a while I read a news story about a little girl asking why she can't do this or that: play Little League baseball, serve on the altar, aspire to be a priest. It cheers me to picture her family supporting her questioning, and gathering together to work out the consequences when they don't find good answers forthcoming from the powers that be. That is a good image for the domestic church, the deep family life that the good news of Jesus solicits. When people join together to ask serious questions and explore the Mystery of why the world is as it is, they push forward as free spirits, show one another how to care for life and love it.

8 *POLITICS*

FEMINISTS AGAINST CHRISTIANS

At its best, politics is our concerted effort to care for life and
love it. Politics derives its name from the Greek city-state
(*polis*), whose members joined in trying to make a common weal, a
conjoint prospering. True, many people were left out of the Greek
political calculus. Women and slaves, for example, did not count
as full members. In the view of many feminists today, the historical
political structures, one and all, owe women, slaves, and other
outsiders sizable recompense. So large is this debt, some feminists
judge, that all our past forms of political arrangement are fit only
for the trash bin.

This judgment can lead to opposition between women whose
first sense of feminism is political and women whose first sense is
religious. That would be a fairly straight-forward opposition, if
one still potentially painful. More complicated is the opposition
between women who are religious in somewhat traditional terms
and women who are religious (or "spiritual") in terms that completely reject traditions such as Christianity. I find myself drawn
to poring over this complexity as an entry-point to "politics."

The women represented in *The Politics of Women's Spirituality*, a
useful reader edited by Charlene Spretnak, speak in tongues that I
must interpret. Sometimes they write paragraphs to which I take
little exception, as, for instance, this by Sheila D. Collins: "Racism,
sexism, class exploitation, and ecological destruction are four in-
terlocking pillars upon which the structure of the patriarchy rests.
The structures of oppression are everywhere the same, although

148

the particular forms in which oppression is manifested may at first glance look different. The democracy of the Athenian *polis*, to which the Western world has always looked as its ideal, was made possible only through the restricted domestic labors of the slaves and wives of the Athenian property owners. Western 'freedom' and affluence depend on the domestication of women and the exploitation of a low-paid labor base made up of minorities and women as well as unlimited access to foreign sources of natural resources which are taken from the ground without regard for the rights of the Earth or the people who live on the land."[1]

I might want to change an adjective or two in that quotation, but I agree with its general analysis. Overall, patriarchy—the rule by males that denies women's equality with men—has spawned societies in which racism, sexism, class exploitation, and ecological destruction are part of the operative machinery, not something on the periphery but something close to the core. It seems to me that these four phenomena seriously call the patriarchal postulate into question. If we can know a political form by its fruits, patriarchy is quite rotten. Were I to find patriarchy an essential part of the American identity, something without which my culture could not function, I would have to give up my American loyalties. Similarly, were I to find patriarchy essential to Christianity, something without which we could not preach the gospel or assemble the communion of saints, I would have to hand in my Christian membership card.

Two paragraphs from another article in *The Politics of Women's Spirituality* make the need for distinctions even more acute. The first paragraph, like the paragraph from Collins, I find unexceptionable. The second paragraph goes against my study, experience, and faith (and so makes me wonder whether I have understood the first paragraph): "The rituals being created today by various women are part of the renaissance of female spirituality, that is, of the ultimate holiness or life-sacredness of women and the female creative process. Within a world which has for centuries tried to brand women as 'unclean,' as 'devils' or as the 'immoral corrupter of man,' this healing process is a vital one.

"It is my belief that *reforming* patriarchal religions, such as Hinduism, Judaism, or Christianity, is not possible, just as reforming capitalism is not possible. The very institutions are contradictory to feminism. Women need to once again create new theory and practices for ourselves in order to reunite the spiritual element with the socio-political,"[2]

The first paragraph points to the undeniable need that many women feel to find themselves as godly as men. Because the traditions have tended to deny women this self-image, new rituals that build a sense of the femininity of the divine are very important. The second paragraph states a conviction for which considerable data could be brought forward, but not a conviction without other data ranged against it. None of the world religious traditions has what I would consider a good record regarding women, but neither has any world religious tradition no appreciation of women's goodness.[3] Such long-lived, complicated entities as Hinduism, Judaism, and Christianity are not purblind. They deal too intimately with daily life to have overlooked completely the contributions of the female half of the membership, the kinship of women with divinity.

So, I find these traditions in principle reformable, possessed of solid hints of a better, non-sexist self. For me a tradition such as Christianity is not only what it has been in the history books written by the patriarchal victors. It is also what has been in the outsiders never much appreciated, the best visions of the saints led by the motherly spirit.

CHRISTIANS AGAINST FEMINISTS

In my view, therefore, the historical reality of the major religious traditions is more complicated than what many radical feminists suggest. The present reality is more complicated, as well, more tangled in its skeins of both oppression and hope. Women in long, vastly extended traditions such as Christianity have done dozens of things, exerted countless influences that rigidly orthodox interpretations might say should have been impossible. They have mediated grace at least as often and as well as men. It is quite possible, on the basis of centrist Christian theological reflection today, to speak of women having been the prime ministers of reconciliation, the likely majority of the *anawim* that Jesus most blessed. This is not to deny that Christianity has been oppressively patriarchal. It is not to diminish by a single whit the need for thoroughgoing reforms. It is simply to say that a historical reading of Christianity that focuses only on the witch burnings and supposedly official exclusions is either ignorant or malicious. The reality has been a great deal more complicated and immensely more reflective of the Lady Wisdom.

The same with the present-day realities. One can only say that a tradition such as Christianity is beyond reformation if one has no confidence in Lady Wisdom, the Holy Spirit, or the work and promise of Jesus Christ. Most radical feminists do indeed have none of these, and so their pessimism is quite logical. But the Christian believer cannot accept such supposed shrewdness from the daughters of this age. She has a different matrimony, quite another inheritance and sense of espousal from God. The Christian God brought the world into being from nothingness. Everything splendid, from babies to seastorms, derives from Her love-life. When we were sinners, this God sent her (his, its) only begotten son to convert us into children of grace.

When I consider what this sort of faith has produced in the saints who have displayed it most vividly, I see hundreds of reasons for hope. Just as the light of one Solzhenitsyn keeps at bay the darkness of an entire totalitarian regime, so the light of one Joan of Arc, Teresa of Avila, or Mother Teresa of Calcutta gives the lie to radical pessimism. It doesn't matter that none of these women is a completely adequate role model for today. That is not the point. The point is that each of these women reached a degree of self-transcendence, signal humanity, that made her an outstanding member of our species. Each pushed her helix far beyond what we average types can make out even when we squint. A "realistic" observer at the time of Joan, Teresa, or Mother Teresa would have given 100-to-1 odds that the woman's dream would come to naught. Yet the woman became a warrior saint, a mystic of the highest order, a Nobel Prize winner and voice of conscience to the world.

"Ah, yes," you may say, "but we 'pessimists' are talking about the religious *institutions*, claiming that institutional Hinduism, Judaism, Christianity and the rest are beyond hope of reform. What you say about individuals does not meet the exact charge." Initially there seems some merit in this rebuttal, but most of it does not stand up to a hard look. First, the charge is hardly exact. In fact, until the proponent makes clear the relation between the institutional form of a religion and that religion's heart and soul, the charge is unusably ambiguous. I could agree, for example, that many of the Christian institutions (Christianity is plural in its institutionality, by no means a monolith) show no likelihood of being reformed to feminist standards. In the cases of the present papacy, Roman Catholic curia, and Eastern Orthodox hierarchy, for instance, the reformer has to make straight for the impossible-to-overestimate powers of the Holy Spirit. In the case of institutions such as the Leadership Conference of Women Religious, signs of hope abound like spring flowers.

Further, Christianity, like Hinduism and Judaism, is much more than its bureaux, dogmas, officials in funny clothing. It is a life-way able to accommodate very diverse sorts of personalities, cultural interpretations of the gospel, symbolic expressions of servanthood and authority. The more than 100,000 grass-roots communities that have sprung up in Brazil alone suggest what inexplicable surgings the Spirit may bring forth. Twenty years ago no one could "reasonably" have predicted that one of the most rigid cultural areas within Christianity would witness such a reform. Parallel phenomena lie ready at hand in Africa and East Asia. There Christianity is growing at a dizzying pace, and constantly calling forth new ritual and doctrinal expression. At the present rate there will soon be more Jesuits from the subcontinent of India than from all the countries of Europe. At the present rate communities in which women exercise liturgical and ministerial roles will soon be a double digit fraction.

One sympathizes with feminists who don't want to deal with such complications as these, who want a simple Christianity they can reject in good conscience, because often such people have a lofty vision and intend a great deal of good. But the realities of the human condition are such that one cannot avoid how things are, actual facts and actual feelings, without soon coming to shipwreck. For radical feminists not to try to understand and find ways of cooperating with women who still find spiritual nourishment in the major religious traditions is to close the door on a dialogue and possible collaboration of enormous moment. So we greatly need protocols for peace among the different feminist wings, and perhaps it devolves on people like me, who stand somewhere near the middle, to think hard about their content.

PEACE

My protocol for peace between such likely antagonistic wings of the feminist movement as radical opponents of Christianity and committed reformers of Christianity begins with a joint examination of the root issues. From the Christian side, I would put forward the request that the rejecting feminists make clear their own solutions for the profound problems of sin, ignorance, and lovelessness. I would also ask them to specify their equivalents to Christian doctrines of God, divinization, and agape, which go beyond therapies for human misery and disclose possibilities for human fulfillment that are strictly supernatural. If we are to have a discussion (with a view to joint action) at the root levels, we have to make clear to one another the heart and soul of our respective religious ventures. What, in fact, are the stances, symbols, rituals we are creating or relying upon to help us deal with life's ineradicable Mystery?

Each tradition ought to try to speak honestly and freshly. Each listener ought to try to clear away the old wax. Christian listeners, for instance, ought to try to hear the deeper overtones of the Goddess religion, the notes that go down to the level of redemption from the worse human evils. They also ought to give the proponents of the Goddess religion more time to develop their still young intuitions. But Christians should not let themselves be shunted away from their own core intuition that, at any level that deserves the adjective "radical," their interlocutor has to come to grips with what has been the central concern of all the great traditions: helping human beings find a proper otherworldliness, a way of coping with evil, beautifying earthly life, and energizing human creativity that points beyond the grave and other ordinary human limitations.[4]

From the feminist side, I would put forward a request that Christians clarify the heart and soul of their religion so as to make it clear what can and cannot be feminized. For example, is it possible for Christianity to reform itself on the foundational level of its doctrines of God, Incarnation, and grace (Karl Rahner's cardinal three), and on the level of ecclesiology (its understanding of the Body of Christ), so as to make femininty coeval with masculinity? If the answer is no, a pessimistic view of Christian reform seems

well-warranted. If the answer is perhaps, we must wait and wonder, no doubt seeking further precision on such important sub-
questions as who would bring about such a sexual equalization
and what sort of promulgations would make it effective. If the
answer is yes, and the explanation of what the reformed conceptualization might look like is plausible, the radical feminist would
have to reconsider her pessimism and think about accepting the
hand of welcome extended to her.

Let me be so bold as to continue this two-way reflection,[5] trying
to flesh out the possibilities for an intellectual rapprochement.
Beginning with a Christian response to the request of my radical
feminist, I would say that the doctrine of God, both one and three,
easily admits of a feminist adaptation. God is beyond the confines
of gender, according to mainstream Christian theology, and one
can infer from this that analogies to God from femininity are as
valid as analogies from masculinity. It is true that Christian Scripture and the Councils have been prone to masculine imagery, but
one can view this as an historical accident (and product of androcentrism). Both Scripture and the Councils so picture the divine
Mystery that feminine imagery is congenial. Thus one could say
"Goddess" as well as "God," speak of the divine as "She" as well as
"He," "Mother" as well as "Father." I have already indicated my
own half-way house: to make the regular referent of the Spirit feminine. But one might also explore the feminine (e.g., womblike)
overtones to the recessive character of the Augustinian Father
(whose analogy is human memory), and to the holistic character
of the Thomist Father (whose analogy is unlimited understanding).

Christology or the implications of the Incarnation poses a different set of problems, but none of these seems insoluble. I think
that Christianity would have to continue to say that the incarnation of the Word in Jesus of Nazareth was unique, but I see no
reason why it could not add that the Word might just as well have
taken flesh in a female form, and that the Christic character of the
members of the Incarnate Word has nothing to do with their masculine or feminine sex. This would imply that women are as much
images and vessels of God as men, and that all offices in the church
ought to be open to both sexes equally. There are historical precedents for a piety that stresses the maternal aspects of Jesus,[6] but
Christians would have to mount a strong campaign to root out the

undeniable psychological consequences of their having spent twenty centuries picturing God's humanity in nearly exclusively male terms. Still, in principle the doctrine of the Incarnation does not have to say that maleness is essential to God's taking flesh. As I understand it, that is never what it said or has been defined to entail.

Grace and ecclesiology are even easier cases. Grace basically means the divine life, and there is nothing exclusively masculine about such agape. The church essentially is the people who open themselves to God's exchanges of love and find their best symbolic "headship" in Christ. There may be political reasons for working delicately with the tradition of male institutional leadership in many sub-traditions, but there is nothing in the cardinal tenets of Christianity that necessitates an all-male clergy, any more than there is anything that necessitates papal infallibility.[7] The good flourishing of many Christian communities that do not accept either necessity shows that they cannot be essential. The only Christian essentials are the things that open a person to the explicit (what Rahner calls the categorical) forms of grace: the inmost forms that build the Christian reality and the Pauline "mind of Christ."

PERSONAL POLITICS

Responding from the radical feminist side, I would stress the ecological and psychological riches of the Goddess tradition. Not only do the rituals through which women (and some men) affirm the sacrality of femininity help to offset the theological depreciations of femininity—which most of recorded history, being androcentric, has sponsored—they also help devotees to relate more peacefully to nature and the fragmented parts of their own psyches. This is very helpful for what one might call "personal" politics: trying to negotiate a consciousness congenial to the helix of freedom and careful love.

The symbol of the Goddess reminds us that many traditions (e.g. Hinduism) have colorfully portrayed the Ultimate as androgynous, male-female. If the Western traditions have tended to stress the transcendence of God, and then to picture God as male (when they have to make this-worldly analogies), the Eastern traditions have tended to use a coincidence of opposites—to point to the mystery of the ultimate reality by throwing together symbols that capture different salient aspects. This has meant that most Hindu gods have had a goddess-consort, and that the folk religion of India has worshipped a Mother-Goddess more than a Vishnu or Shiva. It has meant that the Eastern source of the world has been something like the Buddhist Tathagatagarba: the Womb of the Buddha from which all entities derive. In the case of China, the motherly Tao has played an analogous role.

Ecologically, the Goddess tradition makes it clear that religion can be holistic, integrating, and an opponent of mentalities that alienate human beings from the cosmos. This is in itself a valuable form of salvation. If salvation is the process of making people whole and restoring them to health, rituals that overcome people's alienations from nature can mediate considerable salvation. Similarly, rituals that overcome people's sense of alienation from divinity, themselves, and other human beings are quite definitely soteriological. When the Goddess is portrayed as the mistress of life, the Source as deep and varied as the care and wildness running through the physical world, She is a quite adequate ultimate reality. So much of our well-being depends on a proper relation to nature that one might even speak of a providential return of Goddess themes today. For a time of ecological crisis, when everything from acid rain to nuclear pollution threatens the matrix of all future life, the portrayal of the creative source of the world as a Mother passionate for the well-being of all her offspring is most apposite.

Psychologically, personal peace demands the integration of what Jungian psychology speaks of as the masculine and feminine aspects of the personality, the animus and anima. Both sexes have these aspects, and until either a woman or a man comes to grips with both, the personality does not have the resonance, give, and joy it might. Creative works make special demands on our psychic integrity, and so can occasion the deep connections between our two sides that we need. Similarly, religious rituals can take us below our work-a-day dichotomizing, offer images and experiences that help us *feel* integral. The dances that many Goddess covens employ have the potential, as do the chantings and visualizations.

I think that a dialogue between radical religious feminists and Christian reformers would have to spend considerable time discussing symbolism, myth, and truth, but I have little doubt that they could find themselves complementary. My intuition is that often the radical adherents of the Goddess religion have psychological acuity on their side, while often the reforming Christians have ontological depth. If the two could dream together about a common language,[8] they might overcome many an accidental alienation.

To both sides, this sort of dialogue probably would bring home the importance of breaking free of "ideology" and "dogma." These words can have positive connotations, but here I have negative connotations in mind. When two women speak to one another, they can either put forward positions that they think they must represent, "official" interpretations, or they can stress their personal experiences and convictions (which no doubt have been somewhat shaped by their past allegiances). I very much hope that, in the dialogue I envision, feminists will choose the second option. Feeling free to say what they personally have found valuable in their tradition, and what has yet completely to suit them, they could form an alliance against inauthenticity wherever found, for truth whatever its source. For the fact is that there is cant on both sides, rhetoric broken loose from experiential moorings. Christianity has the special burden of many centuries of abusive treatment of women, so the Christian partner has a special obligation to be painfully honest. Radical feminism is the younger tradition, at least in its present psychological and political forms, so it has a special obligation not to over-simplify, to try to give all the members of the race, past and present, a proper hearing.

The yield of such a personal politics, I suspect, would be still more freedom and careful love. Women who can grant one another an assumption of good will, probe the areas (economic, religious, psychological, educational) in which they almost certainly have suffered similarly, and emerge enriched by testimonials they have to respect (even when they cannot say they understand or agree with them) have taken another turn in their journey, another giant step toward the divinity that is Goodness and Truth.

INSTITUTIONAL POLITICS

The divinity that is Goodness and Truth sets the ground rules for a feminist participation in institutional politics. If the question is,

"How can feminists work in or through unliberated institutional structures?" the answer might well be, "By keeping Goodness and Truth clearly before them." For example, feminists convinced of the overall goodness and truth of the politics and programs of an organization such as NOW (National Organization of Women) can work for those policies and programs in good conscience. Only when they run into policies and programs that they find untruthful or ethically dubious will they have to review their allegiance. If they come to a point where the overall policies and programs seem to be doing more harm than good, or seriously violate their personal consciences, they have to withdraw allegiance. However, as long as the good outweighs the evil and truth overbalances falsity, they can peacefully slog along. To be sure, they have an obligation to use their influence to improve programs and policies they find lacking. Only the purist, though, will feel she must have a group that perfectly mirrors her own convictions.

Let me give an example. Suppose that a woman deeply convinced that most abortions are immoral finds that her best fellow feminists espouse a very different position. Is she obliged to step back from all cooperation with these fellow-workers? Does she have to refuse to join their organizations? I don't think so. It seems to me that as long as this person withholds support for the particular projects she finds unacceptable (for example, sponsoring abortion clinics), and makes her voice heard in general policy discussions, she can continue to work for the organization's other goals, like better sex education, more female candidates for political office, and economic reforms.

Such a policy of selective allegiance seems to me the best way to handle the pluralistic character of most of our contemporary institutions. To those who say that outsiders will misinterpret selective allegiance and put the qualified loyalist down as a wholehearted supporter, I can only respond that all political acts are liable to misinterpretation. The fact is that pluralistic politics is the order of our day, and simple-minded, one-issue politics is not defensible. Much more reprehensible than the person who picks and chooses allegiances as a sophisticated practitioner of "this, but not that," are those who would vote out of office the good public servant who happens to disagree with them on one issue, or withhold support from a good group because one aspect of the group's activities offends their economic, religious, or political sensibilities. The reality of contemporary political life is that an individual can virtually never find a cause or party that has no unobjectionable aspect. We either become sufficiently sophisticated to pick and choose or we become ideologic people who buy a group's platform wholesale (or the notion of nonparticipation), and use it in place of personal thought.

The Christian church is also a political institution, so these reflections apply to it as much as to such secular organizations as NOW or the Democratic party. The base-line question is the same: Does this church, overall, have policies and programs that I find true and good? Can I work in it for the goals I find most pressing while objecting to the goals I find offensive? Do the people I find myself working with bring out the best in me, take me toward the sort of community life, family life, and spirituality I most want? If the answer to these questions is yes, I am fortunate indeed: I have found a spiritual home.

If the Christian church is my spiritual home, I have the right and obligation to try to improve it. For while the traditional models of obedience have something to be said for them, today they clearly need to be supplemented by models that better factor in the contributions of all the church's members. This is especially true regarding women. Women have to look carefully at the Christian church as a whole, and at the particular church they find themselves in, to see whether it is in fact an entity they can support in good conscience. And this applies not only to new members but to women who have grown up in a church without a great deal of critical thought and now find themselves shocked at its sexism. Such women have to make a new decision about their religious community. If they decide that, overall, they can support its programs and policies, they can in good conscience maintain loyal membership, all the while trying to change the policies and programs of which they disapprove.

Finally, I think that feminists can be gradualists, people satisfied with slow but steady progress. No doubt there is a place for impatience, but most change comes rather gradually. Thus I would counsel feminists to keep their eyes on the overall goodness and truth of the institutions they are supporting. If a group continues to ring true, and seems to be making progress, one can make do with a less than breakneck pace. For example, one can support the move to ordain women to the diaconate without giving up one's conviction that this is but a half-way house on the road to full sexual equality in access to religious offices. Similarly, one can keep attending liturgical functions that retain imperfect language and symbolism, as long as they advance the overall goodness that one loves. On occasion, of course, there may be a call for boycott or denunciation. Political life unfolds case by case. But overall one can be a regular participant, as loyal as one is critical.

NATIONAL POLITICS

Because I have been able to affirm the overall goals of my Christian community, all the while speaking out against its failures to live up to its ideals, I have remained a loyal member and judged the church reformable. Neither past history nor present policies have forced me to conclude that the Christian church cannot deal with women as the equals of men. I find a similar judgment forthcoming when I review the history and present policies of my country. The United States is far from a bastion of feminism, but we have witnessed considerable progress in the past two decades. Nothing in principle denies the possibility that women by the year 2025 would hold an equal share of political and economic power. I would not bet the farm on that, but it could in fact happen. So I don't find it necessary to withdraw from national politics or advocate completely scrapping the present system. I think we need a very deep (radical) reform of our economic system and a great deal of work to root out racism and sexism, but I'm not convinced that a completely new beginning would be possible or desirable. Right now that seems to me utopian: it is worth contemplating for the insights it brings, but not something I should give over all I have to try to make happen.

This is not to deny the far-reaching consequences of a feminist vision; its full realization would bring a regime that presently looks utopian. Were we to establish an economy in which being female or a person of color wasn't a penalty, an economy in which people weighed more than profits, an economy and foreign policy that eschewed militarism, and an economy that was ecologically defensible, the result would be both feminist and ideal beyond present likelihoods. Yet each of these changes seems to me implicit in the feminist principles of women's right to equality and women's predilection for care, and any advance toward one of these changes will bring the others closer, for they share an inner linkage.

However, until feminism or some like-minded reform movement overhauls the present institutions of our national polity, women are going to have to be pickers and choosers. We will find ourselves in imperfect situations, forced to select from a much less than full bill of fare. Choices that seem just and reasonable will have failed to make the menu because of pressure groups and special interests. The wealthy will continue to have far more to say than they should. But each time we do the best we can with these imperfect options, and make it known how imperfect they are indeed, we fulfill the obligations of good citizenship. If we cannot afford the time, energy, and money necessary to exert maximum political leverage, we can at least make sure that our political representatives know our feminist views. This can be a discouraging venture in many parts of the country, but I have been surprised to find that even powerful, apparently invulnerable politicians are quite sensitive to their constituents' views.

Need realistic participation in the American political process make one a middle-of-the-roader, or even a conservative? I don't think so. It can make us people in for a long haul of loyal opposition, witnesses whose religious convictions reach to extend a carte blanche to God's strange ways. Concerning peace, for example, I find no option but dogged resistance to militaristic policies. The arguments for strategic deterrence, for instance, seem to me straight out of a manual for hell or a mental hospital. The only sure way to avoid nuclear war is to eliminate nuclear weapons and the conditions under which people would be moved to use them. This is indeed a difficult undertaking, and I can see a place for temporary strategies that depend on a retaliatory capacity.[9] But to have any longterm goal other than moving the human race as far as possible from the psychological as well as technological capacity for nuclear war seems to me deeply immoral.

Among the issues struggling for priority in American national politics, this one of war and peace seems to me primary. It is a cloud on every other horizon: economic, cultural, sexual, and religious. Women have tended to be more disturbed about this issue than men, out of a stronger instinct that our present militarism is dangerous if not crazy. We women have seen a close kinship between the ways that men prepare for war and the ways they run too many businesses and churches. Again and again, power and pride run over common sense. Again and again an "us against them" mentality rules out the possibility of reconciliation or of redefining the problem in terms that make it "all of us in it together."

I doubt that the American generals or diplomats are worse villains than the Soviet, and I have no hesitancy about proclaiming the American system as it now runs a better vehicle for Truth and Goodness than the Soviet system as it now runs. But that is a far cry from proclaiming the present American system something of which a feminist or Christian can be proud. We lie too much, bully too much, and too often pursue unworthy goals such as economic or miltary self-service. We too often profess ideals of democracy and fair play that our foreign behavior mocks. Until we are less hypocritical and come to the bargaining table with cleaner hands, we shall have little moral authority. Moral authority will not win over opponents whose own consciences are shuttered, but it will save our own souls and attract people of good faith. That is the main Christian-feminist agendum I see for national politics: helping our country save its soul, its genuine commitment to Goodness and Truth.[10]

INTERNATIONAL POLITICS

When the discussion of politics reaches the world level, the various world-religious traditions become a significant factor.[11] The feminist voice tends to be under-represented in these traditions, but the majority of them so oppose ruthless capitalism and Marxism that their collective voice is still a strong call for better ways to keep the world's peace and advance the world's justice. The militant fundamentalist faiths (most notably, militant Islam) complicate the picture, but by and large the international religious bodies are on the side of the angels. So, for example, the reports of the World Council of Churches' meeting at the Massachusetts Institute of Technology in 1979 contain a wealth of scientific, economic, technological, political, and religious insights whose cultivation could hasten the day of world-wide justice.[12]

The problem of making peace in the global village is certainly a top priority in any realistic assessment of international politics today, and linked closely with it is the problem of working out a more equitable world-wide economy. Until we solve the disparities between the living standards of the Northern nations and the Southern nations we shall have an imbalance always on the verge of violent conflict. The involvement of the United States in Latin America is perhaps the most relevant domestic example, and it shows how much the Northern nations have to clean up if they are to get their own houses in order.

A third international problem is the rapidly deteriorating world-wide ecology, and I would like to focus briefly on it. Ecological sensitivity has been one of feminists' earliest and deepest characteristics. In speculating on women's ties to nature, the feminist theoretician Carol Christ suggested why:

> Simone de Beauvoir, a theorist of women's experience but not of mysticism, has noted that women often experience a transcendence in nature that is closed to them in society. "As a member of society she enters upon adult life only in becoming a woman; she pays for her liberation by abdication. Whereas among plants and animals she is a human being; she is freed at once from her family and from the males." De Beauvoir rightly calls attention to women's exclusion from culture as one reason for their mystical experiences with nature. It should also be noted that traditional cultural associations of women with nature and the conventional limitation of their sphere to children, home, and garden also encourage women to be open to mystical experiences of nature. In almost all cultures, women's bodily experiences of menstruation, pregnancy, childbirth, and lactation, combined with their cultural roles of caring for children, the sick, the dying, and the dead have led to the cultural association of women with the body and nature, and men with culture, the spirit and transcendence. Whether or not women really are closer to nature than men, cultural attitudes and cultural roles have encouraged women to develop a sense of their own affinity with nature. Poet Susan Griffin, who has explored many aspects of women's feelings of connection to nature, writes, "The earth is my sister; I love her daily grace, her silent daring . . . and I do not forget: what she is to me, what I am to her."[13]

Were we to regard the earth as our sister or mother as hundreds of generations of our forebears did, we might be primed for the spiritual conversions necessary to move international politics in a direction more responsible ecologically. As it is, the economically developing nations seem only to be repeating the follies of the economically developed nations, so that controls on pollution of the air, the waters, and the land alike have become a weird hallmark of affluence. Thus some of the worst pollution occurs in developing cities such as Cubatao, Brazil. Two paragraphs from a recent work on the Christian theology of nature show the confluence of economic exploitation by northern countries and the increasing ecological pollution in the southern hemisphere:

> More precisely, atmosphere tests indicated that each day Cubatao's 50 square mile area was bombarded by about 473 tons of carbon monoxide, 182 tons of sulfur dioxide, 148 tons of particulate matter, 41 tons of nitrogen oxide, and 31 tons of hydrocarbons. The giant factory of the Paulista Steel Company was the largest polluter, but other Brazilian firms, the American firms Dow Chemical, Du Pont, and Union Carbide, and French and German firms all contributed. The pollution of Cubatao therefore has international causes. It is a good example of the complex way Northern technologies and economies are changing the face of Southern landscapes for the worse.
>
> Cubatao has become sufficiently infamous to have made the wire services, and the newspaper report from which I gathered my statistics included some descriptive color: "Smoke rolls forth from scores of stacks in blue, yellow, red, charcoal and white, turning the air a jaundiced gray and invading the nostrils with a sickening mixture of acrid odors. There are no birds and no insects, and when it rains on particularly windless days, the drops burn the skin. The industries of Cubatao have given the city the highest average per capita income of any city in Brazil, but the profits do not reach most of the city's inhabitants. Thirty-five percent live in shanty towns like Vila Parisi with no social services."[14]

It takes only slight imagination to see Brazilian women with burning skin, hovels for homes, and an infant mortality rate more than eight times that of the United States. It takes only slight illation to see that women's traditional affinities for nature have today to become part and parcel of a worldwide lobbying for a new economic, political, and cultural order. When the matrix of life is imperiled by male militarism, greed, and lust for technological control, women have to become the prime defenders of the bed of life. Internationally, feminism can be the vanguard of the earth's preservation.

THE CITY OF GOD/ESS

Were the earth to survive and flourish, we might speak of a city built by a love of divinity that properly honored its feminine aspect. We might speak of a city that was round and beautiful, quiet and harmonious. Doris Lessing has already spoken eloquently of such a city, and I love to recall her description: "The Round City showed nothing that was not round. It was a perfect circle, and could not expand: its bounds were what had to be. The outer walls of the inner buildings made the circle, and the side walls, as I made my way through on a path that was an arc, I saw were slightly curved. The roofs were not flat, but all domes and cupolas, and their colours were delicate pastel shades, creams, light pinks and soft blues, yellows and greens, and these glowed under the sunny sky . . . [It] was thronged, and a healthier friendlier crowd I have never seen. A pervasive good humor was the note of this place, amiability —and yet it was not clamorous or hectic. And I noted that despite the noise a crowd must produce, this did not impinge on the deep silence that was the ground note of this place, the music in its inner self, which held the whole city safe in its harmonies."[15]

It seems to me important to include such atmospheric or environmental details when we put our imaginations to work on the kind of planet we want to inhabit. When women reach for justice,[16] they should strive for the most egalitarian, holistic, and beautiful achievement possible. In this they likely will be reproducing some of the innermost convictions of the Jesus movement, which shows signs of having been radically egalitarian.[17] Feminist theoreticians are also correct to study the helps available in Marxist thought,[18] the great strength of which is its appreciation of the links between economics and class. The deepest Marxist visions, however, become siblings of Christian visions of a just society, so one does not eliminate the mystical by beginning with economics. If economic analysts keep moving on to further questions, they soon contemplate the whole of reality, the mystery of why the current order is as it is.

It is these further questions and our willingness to take them up that determine how spiritual our politics will be. If we are willing to follow the deeper implications of our struggles after justice, we need not divorce such struggles from prayer and deep reflection. True enough, there is always the danger that we will get lost in mere reflection and forget the primacy of praxis (in evangelical as well as Marxist thought). On the other hand, praxis without reflection and prayer is but half a loaf, no nourishment for the full journey. The full journey must provide for bread *and* roses. An artist such as Lessing shows this very clearly. She is appalled at the suffering and ugliness that injustice brings, so early in her career she is an energetic Communist. As she matures, however, she sees the unregenerate character of Stalinist Communism and finds she must move on to something deeper and more honest. In the *Canopus in Argos* volumes this something deeper is the universe's necessity. Ironically, all the while that Lessing lashes out at the established religions for their dogmatisms and cruelties, the core of her work is a deeply religious sense that until we have surrendered to the universe's necessities we shall have no human order, no beauty, justice, or peace.

The paradox at the heart of religion, at the core of human maturation, is the fact that the closer we come to God and the universe's necessities the more free and responsible we become. Human liberty is as Augustine long ago perceived: the freedom to do what we should. We should grow, develop, keep moving upward. We should press ahead without losing our care, but finding cares that are more challenging and refined. But the more fully we develop the fewer illusions we shall have about human freedom. We are the pots, not the potter. We undergo far more than we bring about. Indeed, our mature arts, sciences, and businesses are the bringing about of what ought to be, what is encoded along the osmotic border between us and physical nature. We do not have to color the human commonweal in Lessing's pastel shades, but we do have to color it with good humor, harmony, and music.

That is a failing metaphor, of course, and meant to be. We don't color music, harmony, and humor in any literal sense. Yet we do

perceive humor, harmony, and music as though shaded, chroma-
tic, making an appeal to all our senses. The more holistic our sense
of harmony, for example, the more fully it evokes feelings, scents,
sights, and tastes, as well as sounds. The city properly divine, worthy of self-transcendent women and men, will be sensual, beautiful, akin to the heavenly Jerusalem of Revelation.

Where the city properly divine will differ from the city of Revelation, because of 2000 more years of imagination and a much
heavier feminine contribution, will be in its larger quotient of softness, roundness, and gentleness. The Goddess will have balanced
the warrior God, the maternal principle will have harmonized the
paternal. The strength of enduring, begetting, and suffering will
be as honored as the strength of conquering, hunting, and triumph-
ing. Beyond the eschatological reversal that Jesus depicts, when the
people of the beatitudes have come into their own, we shall see
what might have been in history: people free to love, people growing and careful. The new city of God/ess will not repudiate the old
city of God. It will merely sublate it another turn of the helix. Then
female politicians will finally feel vindicated, sanctioned in their
inalienable instinct that they have always been as necessary and
wise as male politicians, as equally essential to divinization.

9 SUMMARY AND CONCLUSION

THE PROBLEMATIC REVISITED

I began this essay on feminist spirituality with the students in my "Women and Religion" classes to the forefront of my mind. Consistently, I find them seeking a handle on their lives, a spirituality that will help them make sense of their frustrations, get out of their ruts, grow deeper roots and gain broader vistas. At the same time, I find them concerned to preserve values and instincts that seem to them peculiarly feminine: care for life, sympathy for the vulnerable, relationship with as many friends and neighbors as are agreeable. The central problem for my students therefore is a matter of both/and. They want a pathway that will take them forward, stimulate their best energies and creativities without depriving them of their feminine sensitivities.

In working out a model of feminist spirituality as self-transcendence I have simply tried to analyze this both-and petition and answer it, using resources from current Christian feminist reflection. I shall review this reflection and then the model itself momentarily, but here let me linger over the problematic. As I have described it, my students' longing may seem rather knowing, quite well aware of what it is asking. In fact, this is seldom the case. The unknown that my students are pursuing is only known to those few who have had the good fortune to learn how to focus on their drives, discern their emotions, bring clarity to their churning innards. Only rarely in our society has a school or church taught people like my students how to reflect and clarify. Most of the time they are quite confused, much less than collected and well focused. So while one could call what goes on in "Women and Religion" a species of consciousness raising, a better term would be consciousness clarifying. The people I deal with are aware that they suffer many injustices as women and get much less than equal treatment, but they are unaware of the structures of this awareness, its sources and extent.

Dinah Howell, the central character in Robb Forman Dew's fine novel, *Dale Loves Sophie to Death*,[1] is a good middle-class illustration of the women of raised but unclarified awareness. She knows that her forays back to the midwestern town where she was brought up are bound to bring her more pain than pleasure. She would agree that dragging three kids back to that heat and swirl of adolescent emotions each summer is dim or mad, but she cannot help herself. Until she has found whatever it is that she is looking for, that is driving her, she has to continue to confront her strange parents, the old scenes of her formation. Coupled with her lack of forward focus is her failure to develop a career or a cause to absorb her creative energies. Dinah's lack of clarity about the past renders her immobile, dissipated of all energy. There is no helical movement in her life. She is barely able to tread water and many days seems quite likely to go under.

Few of my students show as much ennui as Dinah, but a majority have not got their energy in gear. They are dissipated, fragmented, unfocused. Unclarified trauma from their past, demanding kids and spouses in their present, and they don't-know-what in the future lying ahead confuse them badly about their course. Who are they and where are they going? What do they want to be when they grow up and away from these present impasses? Those are not the overt questions my students put to me or the texts we study. Those are not the overt questions they put to themselves, since they would not know how to begin to answer them. But in fact those are the questions that best express my students' turmoils and worries. Were these women to meet a dazzling shaman, prophet, or sage, those are the questions they would set her to answering.[2]

Dinah's best natural candidate for a sage is her own father, a learned if cold psychiatrist. Her father can only proffer a rather meager comfort, however, his awareness that her life like his own has not been easy: "It's not easy, either, to know that you can't love your children the way they want to be loved. You can only love people however you happen to love them. I *did* always know that you weren't happy and that it would be hard for you, but I always thought that you understood that I don't . . . *enjoy* life either. I hoped you'd give me credit for my own misery. And I hoped that you'd know that I wished you well."[3]

Robb Forman Dew does not despise this meager comfort. Dinah knows that coming from her taciturn father this is a considerable revelation, an unusual forthcomingness. But the reader with religious experience and a theological education will find its barrenness touching. How sad that the vaunted achievements of "man come of age" should boil down to such a joyless little specimen. How ironic that those who felt they had no need of womanish things like Christian faith should in their old age be asking credit for their misery.

Dinah's father seems less than heroically honest, however. If a person has not been able to find a pathway to splendor, joy, peace, and transcendence, he might at least imply that he has missed the boat. Perhaps Dinah's father means to imply such a confession, but I note that he doesn't tell his daughter to look for another spirituality, a pathway different from his own. Rather he implies that there is no pathway to joy, that saints and happy folk are either frauds or simpletons.

Sometimes the best among my students seem to be verging on this judgment. Having rejected the pieties of Bible-belt religion, they think they have no alternative but a cynical secularism. My task with them is to stir up the wellsprings of their consciousness and point out the Mystery that is ineluctable.

THE THEORY REVISITED

To sketch an adequate background for a spirituality that would meet my students' needs, I first went to Rosemary Haughton. Her romantic interpretation of the Christian God's love begets a stunning view of history. In that interpretation, history depends on breakthroughs, times when the divine love can overcome our sinful closures and break us apart and establish exchange on a higher or deeper level. The ways of such a divine love longing to communicate itself are the ways of Lady Wisdom. Wherever there is wholeness, healing, and genuine community, one can speak of her gracious presence. Wherever people prefer poverty, freedom, and creativity to a life wealthy only in worldly terms we can say that she is stirring. Haughton takes seriously the passionate character of God's care for her creation. Lady Wisdom is as far from the God of the Deists, the divine clock-maker, as is Shiva the energetic destroyer.

If we take Haughton's vision to the window and reset our glass, the world looks more dynamic, evolutionary, and adventurous. Human time becomes a wonder-laden pilgrimage, an ongoing exploration. It becomes an erotic romance, not in the sense of daytime television but in the sense of a burning quest for the grail of beauty and truth, Christian love and redemption. The Dinah Howells of the world will find little ennui in Haughton's view of history. Such stasis can only be the pause before the next breakthrough, the rest-hut before the next ascent of the mountain trail. God is always greater than our resistances, persistent and pervasive though our resistances be. The love that moves the stars is always more. When we have a sense of moving out toward what is always more, dealing with a positively infinite Mystery, we begin to realize the importance of "self-transcendence," our birthright to ever more light and love.

Transcendentalist theologians such as Lonergan, Rahner, and Voegelin clarify the dynamics of human consciousness. In their clarifications it becomes clear that reason itself is directional, lured by the divine Mind that makes it lightsome. In Lonerganian judgment the person knows that she is made to know, that knowing is her quintessential operation. In Rahnerian intercourse with the divine Mystery the person knows that her knowledge must lead on to love. Since the real God is always a no-thingness, a fullness overspilling all our capacities, we have to say a yes that goes beyond our knowing and commit ourselves to entailments stretching far beyond our present sight. The Mystery that could be an abysmal void we believe to be the horizon of our spirituality, the backdrop that makes all our knowing and loving possible. The Christ-event that we make the center of history is our warrant for such an audacious faith. Because of Jesus of Nazareth whom God raised from the dead, our drives to know and love can expect fulfillment. Indeed, beyond any fulfillment owed to us, Jesus' God has chosen to establish exchanges that work our divinization.

The feminist theoreticians whom I have found most helpful accept the model of development and ongoingness, but point out the historical liabilities under which women's development has labored. Because most times and places have feared ongoing women and branded them as pushy or uppity, women have inherited a socialization to timidity, passivity, and self-sacrifice. Their psychological profile, as studies such as Gilligan's have shown, locates growth and development in more careful enterprises, ways of solving problems and getting work done that are holistic, relational, concerned to give all parties their due. Often this makes women's moral lives unbearably complex, overloaded with feelings of obligation. The result is torpor such as Dinah Howell's, a sense that it's just too much to handle. Thus a shocking number of the subjects in Gilligan's abortion group seem to have drifted into their predicaments. They feel both guilty and dead-ended, damned if they do and damned if they don't. Not only have the men to whom they have been related badly let them down, they have badly let themselves down and not had the ego strength to handle their fertility as they themselves have wanted.

My theoreticians therefore suggest a sophisticated analysis of women's consciousness. On the one hand, there are the drives to know, love, work creatively, and help bring about social justice. On the other hand, there are the sensitivities to relationships, holistic gestalts, and paying special heed to the human factors in problematic situations. If women are not to feel denatured, such species of care have to retain their viability. If we are not to feel frustrated, such species of care cannot mean a love of neighbor that shortchanges the self, a sense that one has been born to be a servant or victim. And, complicating the development of both sides of a feminist spirituality, are the legacies of a sinful history: The 62-cent female dollar, being on the margin of most power structures, and being underrepresented in both Congress and the Godhead all tend to give women an inferiority complex.

When women come together in support groups we often find ourselves working to change neural patterns that have deepened through tens of centuries of subordination. As we discover the similarities in our stories, the theories of liberation start to take flesh. Then the concrete job, family problem, religious aspiration and the like which have been troubling me become test cases for God's love. Can the Lady Wisdom illumine even my confusedness? Does the divine will to divinize operate even at 353 Elm Drive? When I can believe that it does, I can speak of good news indeed.

THE MODEL REVISITED

Using the work of Gilligan and Robert Kegan, I have symbolized my adaptation of transcendentalism as a helix of ongoing growth. The helix or upward spiral has two sides of forces. Balancing and pushing against one another, they generate an ascending isometricism. The two forces are the freedom that predominates in the self-assertive aspects of personality development and the care that predominates in the receptive and relational aspects. I want to claim both for women (and men), arguing that their proper correlation makes for an ideal personality development and religious faith. Both call the person beyond her present attainments. Both are the enemy of any wrongful tendency to squat down in present achievements and make "here" a lasting city. The "feminine" side of care assures that here not be a hovel, the present order receive its due. The "masculine" side of pressing forward assures that challenges keep making life interesting, all the works that remain to be done continue to lure us on.

And, of course, the model soon shows that sexual stereotypes are of very limited usefulness. It may be a woman who is pushing forward the claims of the poor and the marginalized. It may be a man who is feeling himself stretched and his present conception of things painfully extended by the demands upon his care. We can go forward because of our own vision, or we can be pushed and pulled ahead by the needs of others. The love of God with whole mind, heart, soul and strength can lure us into deep prayer and service. The love of neighbor as self can put a sharp edge on all our relationships, heat up all our obligations to care. How do we grow, develop, and pursue a fruitful spiritual path? The person in love as Jesus' twofold command directs, marrying freedom to care, can hardly count the ways.

In all the ways that deserve the adjective "feminist," the equality of the sexes as recipients of the good news, ministers of the good news, power-bearers in the community gathered by the good

news will be signal. If the good news is to go to the core of our dis-
eased human condition and give us new hearts of flesh, it must
make us a community of equals. Nowhere is this community more
crucial and intimate than in the relationships between women
and men. Patriarchal marriages, churches, business structures,
and the rest stand as major stumbling blocks on the way to the gospel's realization. By denying the equality of the sexes and making
the female half of the race the second sex, they say that God is not
imaged by all the people equally but has preferential loves that
disfavor one kind. That sort of God won't do today, if indeed it did
in any day. Today, and most any other day, all the people have to
feel that the ultimate reality cares for them as much as for any
other fellow-human.

Among feminist reflectors on this egalitarian thrust of the good
news, I have found an admirable tendency to make it bear on the
equalization not just of women with men but also of the poor with
the rich, the socially unacceptable with the socially esteemed, sinners with the righteous. As Jesus himself conceived it, the Kingdom
of God leveled all vicious oppositions. Horizontally, the parenthood of God meant the siblinghood of all human beings. Verti-
cally, the call of God to one and all made them fit vessels of divine
life. I would therefore make it clearer than I have yet seen it in
Jewish and Christian feminist writings that the Kingdom of God
should today be translated so as to write off all the pejorative possibilities in "election." If one is to speak of an egalitarian community and the demise of all androcentrism, one should also speak of
the universality of the divine offer of grace, the limitless outreach
of salvation.

How we are to square this with a historical dependence on Jesus
the child of Israel is not my present project. Contrary to many, I
find Karl Rahner's notion of anonymous Christianity quite acceptable.[4] One might wish for different language to avoid any hint of
triumphalism, but the core idea that all who accept the mystery of
God can be fitted to Christ's lineaments seems to me to ring deep
and true. It goes to the foundations that any profound spirituality
must reach, and it makes "self-transcendence" synonymous with
fulfillment by the grace of God. Thus what feminists are doing in
their helical advances has analogues, perhaps even identities,
with the progress of any people gambling their lives on truthful-

ness and love. The Christ-event has a fully historical and cultural side, because the Word fully entered into our human condition. But it also has a universal, trans-cultural side, if we accept the Christian belief that the eternal Logos was the divine personhood (not the human personality) of Jesus.

A feminist Christology has to work both sides of this hypostatic relationship, doing justice to both the below and the above. When it does, it should find that its helical model and incarnate divinity are both applicable to each and all. As women who seize their freedom and listen to their care do not do anything essentially different than fully maturing men, so Jews and Christians who live out the Shema and Creed do not do anything essentially different than any other people, explicitly religious or only implicitly, who love divinity and humanity wholeheartedly. The cultural and psychological aspects of each venture will differ, and those differences are terribly important. But in the end, at the center, we are all absolutely equal: all creatures and sinners in need of a grace that comes from a God/ess who has all the priority.

PRACTICE REVISITED

To engage the model with the actual circumstances of people such as my students in "Women and Religion," I have spent four chapters on the zones or sets of preoccupations that seem to me most crucial for a fully adequate feminist spirituality. These zones are prayer, work, family life, and politics. Each topic suggests a dimension of human potential waiting to be actualized. Each names an area of objective reality with which any adequate lifeway must deal.

Prayer is both private and social, both freeing and demanding in terms of care. When people come to a properly contemplative prayer, a way of abiding in God, they actualize the rich possibilities in "divinization" and "covenant." Slowly God and God/ess become almost casually real for them, as objective as the chairs in their living room. This takes some time and help from the Spirit, of course, and it never eliminates the divine Mystery. We remain creatures of flesh and blood, spirits whose natural habitat is material. So much of our best contemplation uses icons or words that

engage our senses in our spirit's longings. Much of our best communal prayer moves through liturgies with fine music and color.
Women often have a strong hunger for deep prayer, and a special
aptitude. As more studies of prayer reflect feminist findings, we
can expect more women to feel at home at their religious depths.[5]

Work is very prominent in the spiritual struggles of many women,
especially those coming back to school or entering the job market
after a decade of childrearing. Despite the progress made toward
lifting women's liabilities at work, economic equality remains a
distant dream. As well, sexual harassment sours many work situations, and many others fail to take women's work-ways into account. So the exchanges many women have with their superiors,
peers, and subordinates are not the exchange Rosemary Haughton
has in mind. Something taints too many of these relationships,
keeps them from the colleagueship and friendship they initially
portend. Call that something closure, original sin, fear of intimacy,
or what you like, it is a dark shadow on a majority of offices. As a
result, the artful side of work, its nisus to become the source of
products both lovely and helpful, can go into eclipse, making the
penitential side, the sweat of one's brow and hurt of one's feelings,
all too prominent. It is not hard to suggest better theories of work,
but in the United States they all run up against the capitalist ethic.
That ethic says that profits can outweigh people, and that the daily
experience of workers is less significant than the accountant's bottom line. So work will not become what feminist intuition knows
it ought to be until capitalist ethics is subverted. On that day the
worker's freedom and care could come forth like a resurrected
savior, telling one and all how foolish and slow of heart they were
not to believe what the prophets of good work had foretold.

Family life holds some of our strongest joys and some of our
sharpest pains, so family life is a high priority in any serious spirituality. Until the relations that most shape our own maturity and
the psyches of the next generation come into evangelical measures
of freedom and care, the cause of our leaving father and mother
will remain obsure. In venturing to marry and generate a family,
we take the challenge of the God of the thornbush to heart. He has
said that he will be as he is with us, as time shows him to have
been. People who marry in this framework become fellow sojour-
ners. Trying to breast each wave of experience as it comes, they

and their offspring trust that it brings them the love of the divine ocean. In the spouses' friendship and parental love, the eros, philia, and agape of Christianity's Hellenistic origins struggle to pull in tandem. By the time that parents have come to middle age, can see their children's children, these loves should have generated a sense of at-home-ness in the world, membership of one another, and ecclesial loyalty. For her own strange reasons, God has gathered us together, tried to make us people, taken us into the divine love-life as branches of her vine. So as we come in sight of death we should feel surging within us unexpected intensities of compassion and love. Such as they have been, our family lives have been necessary, akin to the biblical "did it not have to be?" If we have become freer and freer through our comminglings, and more and more caring, we can say that our creations, like God's, have proven very good.

Politics is the fourth realm in which I tried to imagine some of the implications and applications of my feminist helix. For relations between radical feminists and Christians, between members of the same institution, citizens of the same country, and countries of the one world, the sense of mutual purpose and need a deep spirituality offers is of inestimable moment. For the peace-making needed to avert the nuclear cloud, for the justice needed to offset our demonic economico-political arrangements, and for the preservation of the ecological matrix, feminists need to associate with all people of good will. If this means a politics of both/and, a sophistication that moves far beyond single-issuism, so be it. Surely we ought to be able to muster such minimal maturity. In the city of the god/ess, where feminist instincts will have come fully into their own, maturity will likely be a colorful freedom, a round sort of care, the realization finally that male and female She created us.

L'ENVOI

My parting word could come from Saint Teresa of Avila: Let nothing disturb you. To embark on a spiritual journey is to place oneself in a certain peril, a certain surety of meeting dragons. The only way to keep going, not give up when one sees what beasts inhabit one's own depths as well as the jungles of the world, is to believe that one's God has commanded the quest. By making us as She has, people burning to grow, the God/ess has sanctioned the journey, even the bumps and losses. Surely this is part of what Paul had in mind when he told the Romans that nothing can separate us from the love of God. Surely this is the mutual carte blanche, God's to us and ours to God, at the heart of the saints' special passages. Let nothing disturb you, because everything can work unto your good. Let nothing disturb you, because your disturbance or peace is hardly the final issue. The final issue is your praise and service of God, which you can accomplish grimy or clean, peaceful or agitated.

Too often we cling to a perfectionist God, even when we have known for some time that our best human relationships are not perfectionist. As we do not expect our kids to stay immaculate, as we know that their growth implies trial and error, so God must not expect immaculate performances from us, for we too must keep growing to the time we last take breath. It is far more important that we pick ourselves up and keep going than that we never besmirch our wimple. It is far better to have sinned and repented than never to have wanted or felt. If God cares more for one sinner wandering the path of destruction than ninety-nine saints safe on the way, God cares for even us—you, me, and all the others who show such little faith. It must be that way, if God is not a poor artist, a mother grown stupid or callous.

As Alice Walker especially has seen, God wants our response and admiration, and people who have been beaten down, come to feel low, tend to realize this far better than people moving well.[6] So the experience of black and third world peoples includes moments of amazing grace, notes the previous score gave no cause to anticipate.[7] A spring day brings an ineffable loveliness, and once again redemption seems possible. A spoiled child comes to her senses, washing away years of hurt. In these special moments something of the exchange that God always wants, the passsion God always intends, breaks through our doubts and torpor. Nothing ought to disturb us because our fates finally are more God's than our own.

Therefore, Loyola inferred, we should pray as if everything depended on ourselves (which means praying from very sore need) and work as if everything depended on God. We should do our level best to rout idolatry in all forms, including pernicious worry. If it is our destiny to fail after we have tried our best, it is our obligation to say amen. This is neither defeatism nor quietism. It is merely the proper submission of the creature to the Creator, the Muslim to her Allah.

I know this will be misunderstood, but by my own Teresian advice I cannot let that worry me. Christ was misunderstood, for far less cause or reason. Most of us still live far too much in the eyes of other people, pay public opinion far too much regard. I know there is a good side to public opinion, and I know that women have made it one of their few effective defenses against patriarchal abuse. But I also observe a lot of restricted freedom, a lot of manipulated care, directly traceable to an overconcern for what other people think.

Any adequate conception of society or the church makes a large place for the diversity of the members, the complementarity of their different gifts. If all must walk in lockstep we have no commune worthy of the God/ess. So we should speak and act quite freely, doing our best to serve the God/ess rather than men. We should leave Mammon far behind. Having done our best to be honest and loving, we should let the chips fall where they may. The final accounting is out of our hands anyway, as though God wanted to be sure the General Judgment would be interesting.

Little boys sometimes have heard that winning is the only thing, that a tie is like kissing your sister. In these later days they have also started to hear, at least now and then, that it's how they play the game that matters. Little girls and older women need to make their own peace with this latter dictum. Do we have enough faith that Lady Wisdom gives the increase to follow her ways and let be what will? Can we scrap and lobby and pressure without becoming narrow pagans, people with no better hope than economic or political advantage? I hope that we can and that our spirituality will help us.

We should want to win justice, fairness, women's equal access to every decent creativity, service, and power. We should have a hunger and thirst for righteousness than nothing but God's Kingdom can allay. But we should also keep before us the poor Christ, the defeated Christ, the Messiah who came to grief because of so many false expectations. *This* was the power and wisdom of God, the lifeway found worthy of resurrection. This was the cause of the gospel, the good news, the hopes for divinization now and complete fulfillment in the Kingdom.

Come victory or come defeat, God and Lady Wisdom can turn things to our credit. We have merely to keep going, keep ascending, in ever wider circles of freedom and care. The Spirit promises her help. She groans in our wordless yearning. How, then, can we fail to transcend the old patriarchal order? How can our helix not take us home?

NOTES

Chapter 1: Introduction

1. See Denise Lardner Carmody and John Tully Carmody, *Ways to the Center: An Introduction to World Religions*, 2nd edition (Belmont, CA: Wadsworth, 1984).

2. See, for example, Carol P. Christ, *Diving Deep and Surfacing: Women Writers on Spiritual Quest* (Boston: Beacon, 1980); *The Polititics of Women's Spirituality*, ed. Charlene Spretnak (Garden City, NY: Doubleday, 1982).

3. Robertson Davies, *Fifth Business* (New York: Penguin, 1970); *The Manticore* (New York: Penguin, 1972); *World of Wonders* (New York: Penguin, 1975).

4. *Fifth Business*, p. 65.

5. Ibid., pp. 47–48.

Chapter 2: A Vision

1. Rosemary Haughton, *The Passionate God* (Ramsey, NJ: Paulist, 1981), pp. 276–77.

2. See especially Charles Williams, *Taliessin Through Logres* (New York: Oxford University Press, 1938); *The Descent of the Dove* (London: Longmans Green, 1939).

3. See, for example, Karl Rahner, *Theological Investigations, XVI: Experience of the Spirit: Source of Theology* (New York: Seabury/Crossroad, 1979).

4. Walter Kasper, *Theology of Christian Marriage* (New York: Crossroad, 1983), p. 65.

5. Rosemary Haughton, *The Passionate God*, p. 293. I have read "shows as simultaneously" as a printing mistake (there are many in this edition) and changed it to "shows us simultaneously."

6. See *The Challenge of Basic Christian Communities*, ed. Sergio Torres and John Eagleson (Maryknoll, NY: Orbis, 1981).

7. Robertson Davies, *The Rebel Angels* (New York: Viking, 1982), p. 38.

8. See John Carmody, *The Heart of the Christian Matter* (Nashville: Abingdon, 1983).

9. See Haughton, *The Passionate God*, pp. 279–323.

10. Doris Lessing, *The Sentimental Agents* (New York: Alfred A. Knopf, 1983), p. 95.

Chapter 3: On Self-Transcendence

1. Bernard Lonergan, *Insight* (New York: Philosophical Library, 1957).

2. Bernard Lonergan, *Method in Theology* (New York: Herder and Herder, 1972), p. 103.

3. Ibid., p. 105.

4. See James W. Fowler, *Stages of Faith* (San Francisco: Harper & Row, 1981), pp. 199–211.

5. Jean Auel's novel *The Clan of the Cave Bear* (New York: Bantam, 1981) does a good job at recreating this likely consciousness of early humanity, as does Björn Kurtén's *Dance of the Tiger* (New York: Berkeley Books, 1981). For equivalents among recent shamanic

peoples see Florinda Donner, *Shabono* (New York: Delacorte, 1982), and Michael Harner, *The Way of the Shaman* (San Francisco: Harper & Row, 1980).

6. Eric Voegelin, *Order and History*, vol. 4 (Baton Rouge, LA: Louisiana State University Press, 1974), pp. 189–90.

7. Ibid., p. 246. See Kenneth Keulman, "The Tension of Consciousness: The Pneumatic Differentiation," in *Voegelin and the Theologian*, ed. J. Kirby and W. Thompson (New York: Edwin Mellen, 1983), pp. 61–103.

8. Karl Rahner, *Foundations of Christian Faith* (New York: Seabury/Crossroad, 1978), p. 54. See *A World of Grace*, ed. Leo J. O'Donovan (New York: Seabury/Crossroad, 1980), for interpretive essays that clarify many rough spots in *Foundations of Christian Faith*.

9. See Monika K. Hellwig, *Jesus: The Compassion of God* (Wilmington, DL: Michael Grazier, 1983).

10. Kasper, *Theology of Christian Marriage*, p. 50.

11. Michael Polanyi, *Personal Knowledge* (New York: Harper Torchbooks, 1964), pp. 205–6.

12. Robertson Davies, *The Manticore* (New York: Penguin Books, 1972), p. 119.

13. Robert Kegan, *The Evolving Self* (Cambridge, MA: Harvard University Press, 1982), p. 243.

Chapter 4: Feminist Shadings

1. Carol Gilligan, *In a Different Voice* (Cambridge, MA: 1982), p. 28.

2. See ibid., p. 7ff., which stresses the work of Nancy Chowdorow.

3. See *Women and Analysis*, ed. Jean Strause (New York: Grossman/Viking, 1974), pp. 291–340.

4. See, for example, Judith Plaskow, *Sex, Sin and Grace* (Washington, D.C.: University Press of America, 1980).

5. See Dorothy Dinnerstein, *The Mermaid and the Minotaur* (New York: Harper & Row, 1976).

6. See *Women of Spirit*, eds. Rosemary Ruether and Eleanor McLaughlin (New York: Simon & Schuster, 1979).

7. Barbara Pym, *Excellent Women* (New York: E.P. Dutton, 1978), p. 112.

8. See Gilligan, *In a Different Voice*, pp. 71–127.

9. Rosemary Radford Ruether, *Sexism and God-Talk* (Boston: Beacon Press, 1983), pp. 70–71.

10. Steven S. Schwarschild, "Justice," in *Jewish Values*, ed. Geoffrey Wigoder (Jerusalem: Keter, 1974), p. 1974.

11. See José Miranda, *Marx and the Bible* (Maryknoll, NY: Orbis, 1974).

12. See Ruether, *Sexism and God-Talk*, pp. 47–71; Christine Downing, *The Goddess* (New York: Crossroad, 1981).

13. See Elaine Pagels, *The Gnostic Gospels* (New York: Random House, 1979).

14. Elisabeth Schüssler Fiorenza, *In Memory of Her* (New York: Crossroad, 1983), p. 347.

15. See ibid., pp. 97–241.

Interlude

1. See Starhawk (Miriam Simos), *The Spiral Dance* (San Francisco: Harper & Row, 1979).

2. See Lawrence S. Cunningham, *The Catholic Heritage* (New York: Crossroad, 1983), pp. 170–75 (on Dorothy Day), 197–200 (on Simone Weil).

3. See Mary Daly, *Gyn/Ecology* (Beacon: Beacon Press, 1978).

4. See Elisabeth Schüssler Fiorenza, *In Memory of Her*, pp. 22–26.

Chapter 5: Prayer

1. See Eric Voegelin, *Order and History*, vol. 4, pp. 7–11.

2. See Rosemary Haughton, *The Passionate God*, p. 312.

3. Huub Oosterhuis, *Your Word Is Near* (New York: Newman Press, 1968), pp. 2–3.
4. Yves Congar, *I Believe in the Holy Spirit*, vol. 1 (New York: Seabury, 1983), pp. 9–10.
5. See George A. Maloney, *A Theology of Uncreated Energies* (Milwaukee: Marquette University Press, 1978).
6. Teresa of Avila, *Interior Castle*, as quoted in *A Guide to Prayer for Ministers and Other Servants*, ed. Reuben P. Job and Norman Shawchuck (Nashville: The Upper Room, 1983), p. 27.
7. Simone Weil, *Waiting for God*, as quoted in ibid., p. 36.
8. See *The Way of a Pilgrim*, trans. R.M. French (New York: Seabury, 1965).
9. See Sergius Bolshakoff and M. Basil Pennington, *In Search of True Wisdom* (Garden City, NY: Doubleday, 1979).
10. See Andrew Louth, *The Origins of the Christian Mystical Tradition* (Oxford: Clarendon Press, 1981); Vladimir Lossky, *The Mystical Theology of the Eastern Church* (Crestwood, NY: St. Vladimir's Seminary Press, 1976).
11. See Kurt Weitzmann, et al., *The Icon* (New York: Alfred A. Knopf, 1982), p. 55.
12. Dietrich Bonhoeffer, *The Martyred Christian*, ed. Joan Winmill Brown (New York: Macmillan, 1983), p. 170.

Chapter 6: Work

1. See E.F. Schumacher, *Good Work* (New York: Harper & Row, 1979); Herman E. Daly, ed., *Toward A Steady-State Economy* (San Francisco: W.H. Freeman, 1973); Barbara Ward, *Progress for a Small Planet* (New York: W.W. Norton, 1979).
2. See Robert L. Heilbroner, *Marxism: For and Against* (New York: W.W. Norton, 1980).
3. Robert Coles and Jane Hallowell Coles, *Women of Crisis* (New York: Delta/Seymour Lawrence, 1978), p. 83.
4. See *Women and the Workplace*, ed. Martha Blaxall and Barbara Reagan (Chicago: University of Chicago Press, 1976).
5. See James H. Cone, *Spirituals and the Blues* (New York: Seabury, 1972).
6. Studs Terkel, *Working* (New York: Pantheon Books, 1974), p. xxiv.

Chapter 7: Family Life

1. See John Carmody, *Toward a Holistic Spirituality* (Ramsey, NJ: Paulist, 1983).
2. See Denise Lardner Carmody and John Tully Carmody, *Becoming One Flesh* (Nashville: The Upper Room, 1984).
3. See Joan Meyer Anzia and Mary G. Durkin, *Marital Intimacy: A Catholic Perspective* (Kansas City, MO: Andrews and McMeel, 1980).
4. See the special issue of the *Journal of Ecumenical Studies* on marriage (21:1984).
5. Karol Wojtyla, *Love and Responsibility* (New York: Farrar, Straus & Giroux, 1981), pp. 282–83.
6. See Mary Durkin, *Love Feast* (Chicago: Loyola University Press, 1983).
7. Anne Tyler, *Searching for Caleb* (New York: Alfred A. Knopf, 1975), p. 60.
8. Ibid., pp. 59–60.
9. See John Carmody, *The Progressive Pilgrim* (Notre Dame, IN: Fides/Claretian, 1980).
10. Anne Tyler, *Dinner at the Homesick Restaurant* (New York: Berkeley Books, 1983), pp. 52–53.
11. Note the inter-generational theme in Robert McAfee Brown, *Creative Dislocation–The Movement of Grace* (Nashville: Abingdon, 1980). See also Kathleen and James McGinnis, *Parenting for Peace and Justice* (Maryknoll, NY: Orbis, 1981).
12. See Edward Conze, *Buddhist Wisdom Books* (New York: Harper Torchbooks, 1972).
13. Robert Coles, *Privileged Ones* (Boston: Atlantic-Little Brown, 1977), pp. 552–53.

Chapter 8: Politics

1. Sheila D. Collins, "The Personal Is Political," in *The Politics of Women's Spirituality*, ed. Charlene Spretnak (Garden City, NY: Doubleday, 1982), p. 363.
2. Anne Kent Rush, "The Politics of Feminist Spirituality," ibid., p. 384.
3. See Denise Lardner Carmody, *Women and World Religions* (Nashville: Abingdon, 1979).
4. See John Bowker, *The Sense of God* (Oxford: Clarendon Press, 1973).
5. See Denise Lardner Carmody, *Feminism and Christianity: A Two-Way Reflection* (Nashville: Abingdon, 1982).
6. See Caroline Walker Bynum, *Jesus as Mother: Studies in the Spirituality of the High Middle Ages* (Berkeley: University of California Press, 1982).
7. For an essentialist reading of Christianity that makes a strong distinction between cardinal and secondary doctrines, see John Carmody, *The Heart of the Christian Matter* (Nashville: Abingdon, 1983).
8. See Adrienne Rich, *The Dream of a Common Language* (New York: W.W. Norton, 1978).
9. See John H. Barton, *The Politics of Peace: An Evaluation of Arms Control* (Stanford, CA: Stanford University Press, 1981).
10. See John A. Coleman, *An American Strategic Theology* (Ramsey, NJ: Paulist, 1982).
11. See, for example, Joseph Gremillion and William Ryan, eds., *World Faiths and the New World Order* (Washington: The Interreligious Peace Colloquium, 1978).
12. See Roger C. Shinn and Paul Abrecht, eds., *Faith and Science in an Unjust World*, 2 vols. (Philadelphia: Fortress, 1980).
13. Carol Christ, *Diving Deep and Surfacing* (Boston: Beacon Press, 1980), p. 22.
14. John Carmody, *Ecology and Religion* (Ramsey, NJ: Paulist, 1983), p. 4.
15. Doris Lessing, *Shikasta* (New York: Alfred A. Knopf, 1979), pp. 31–32.
16. See Mary P. Burke, *Reaching for Justice* (Washington: Center of Concern, 1980).
17. See Elisabeth Schüssler Fiorenza, *In Memory of Her* (New York: Crossroad, 1983), pp. 118–30.
18. See, for instance, Carol A. Mackinnon, "Feminism, Marxism, Method, and the State: An Agenda for Theory," *Signs* 7/3 (Spring 1982), 515–44.

Chapter 9: Summary and Conclusion

1. Robb Forman Dew, *Dale Loves Sophie to Death* (New York: Penguin, 1982).
2. See Denise Lardner Carmody and John Tully Carmody, *Shamans, Prophets, and Sages* (Belmont, CA: Wadsworth, 1984).
3. Robb Forman Dew, *Dale Loves Sophie to Death*, p. 215.
4. See Karl Rahner, *Theological Investigations*, XIV (New York: Seabury, 1976), pp. 280–94; *Theological Investigations*, XVI (New York: Seabury, 1979), pp. 194–224.
5. See Mary E. Giles, ed., *The Feminist Mystic* (New York: Crossroad, 1982).
6. See Alice Walker, *The Color Purple* (New York: Washington Square, 1982).
7. See Margaret B. White and Robert N. Quigby, eds., *How the Other Third Lives* (Maryknoll, NY: Orbis, 1977).